MIXED-MEDIA
JOURNALS

D1229235

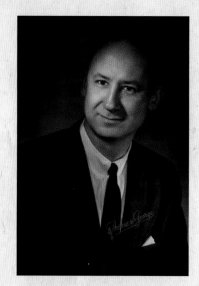

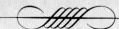

This book is dedicated to
my father-in-law,
Kenneth T. Aimone,
who always reminded me that
"everything is beautiful."

1921–2006

MIXED – MEDIA JOURNALS

Creatively Chronicling Your Life

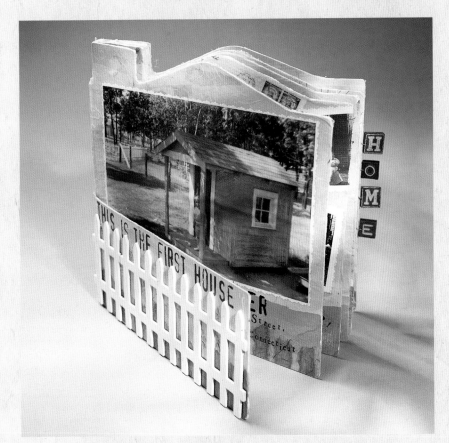

Katherine Duncan Aimone

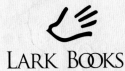

LARK BOOKS

A Division of Sterling Publishing Co., Inc.

New York / London

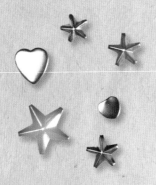

Art Director: Dana Irwin
Assistant Art Director: Lance Wille
Editorial Assistance: Delores Gosnell
Art Interns: Amelia Hancock,
Courtney Tiberio
Photographer: Keith Wright
Cover Designer: Chris Bryant

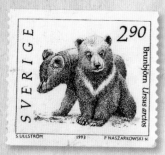

10 9 8 7 6 5 4 3 2 1

Published by Lark Books, A Division of
Sterling Publishing Co., Inc.
387 Park Avenue South, New York, NY 10016

First Paperback Edition 2009
© 2006, Lark Books

Previously published as The Adventurous Scrapbooker: Creating Wonderful Scrapbooks from
Almost Anything

Distributed in Canada by Sterling Publishing,
c/o Canadian Manda Group, 165 Dufferin Street
Toronto, Ontario, Canada M6K 3H6

Distributed in the United Kingdom by GMC Distribution Services,
Castle Place, 166 High Street, Lewes, East Sussex, England BN7 1XU

Distributed in Australia by Capricorn Link (Australia) Pty Ltd.,
P.O. Box 704, Windsor, NSW 2756 Australia

The written instructions, photographs, designs, patterns, and projects in this volume are intended for
the personal use of the reader and may be reproduced for that purpose only. Any other use, especially commercial use, is forbidden under law without written permission of the copyright holder.

Every effort has been made to ensure that all the information in this book is accurate. However,
due to differing conditions, tools, and individual skills, the publisher cannot be responsible for any
injuries, losses, and other damages that may result from the use of the information in this book.

If you have questions or comments about this book, please contact:
Lark Books
67 Broadway
Asheville, NC 28801
828-253-0467

Manufactured in China

All rights reserved

ISBN 13: 978-1-57990-728-0 (hardcover) 978-1-60059-476-2 (paperback)

For information about custom editions, special sales, premium and corporate purchases, please
contact Sterling Special Sales Department at 800-805-5489 or specialsales@sterlingpub.com.

CONTENTS

Introduction 6

Becoming an Adventurous Storyteller 8

Supplies and Tools 8

Working with Photos 14

Planning and Improvising 16

Thinking Outside the Box 18

The Projects 20

Remember 21

This Is the First House 22

A Lifetime of Love 26

My Grandmother's Long Life 30

A Boy's Life 34

Grandmother's Voyage to Israel 38

Snapshots of My Life 42

School Daze 45

My Family's Musical Journey 48

Explore 51

"Dios de la Muerte" Memory Book . . . 52

Doors of Prague 56

Rwanda 2005 60

When In Rome! 63

Nostalgic Grand Mesa Vacation 66

Adventurous Camp Days 69

The Adventures of
    Claudine and George 72

Celebrate 75

Girl's Fantasy 76

Festive Holiday Album 80

Bewitching Paper Doll Book 84

Paper Bag Birthday Book 87

Altered Heart Chapbook 90

Felted Wool Baby Album 93

Sports CD Book 96

Share 99

Nostalgic Friendship Book 100

Fiona's First Year 104

Love Letter to a Garden 107

Bride's Portable Planning Book 110

"UniverSOUL" Circus 113

A Family Gathered 116

Kitsch Kitchen Album 120

Pet Service Tag Book 124

Metric Conversion Chart 127

About the Artists 127

Index 128

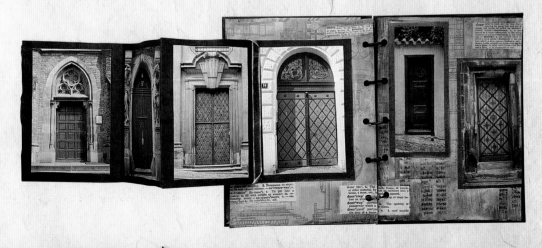

INTRODUCTION

"The future of creative journaling is boundless. A busy mother with no time to 'play' takes up scrapbooking, driven by a desire to document her children's lives and make something she hopes will become an heirloom. As a result, something very creative is awakened in her, and suddenly…the sky's the limit! More and more, I believe this open-minded spirit will encourage journalers to explore their creativity in ways they never dreamed possible."

—LINDA WARYLN

The world of creative journaling is, indeed, *wide open*. This book puts a creative twist on this art by introducing you to the concept of using unusual materials and substrates to enliven your work in this fascinating medium. Venturing outside the box is exciting, stimulating, and even contagious!

Thirty projects, all certain to inspire you, are created by artists who love making journals but also work in other media, such as collage, bookmaking, graphic design, fiber art, or polymer clay. Whether you're an avid paper crafter, a diligent journaler, an altered-art visionary, or a mixed-media magpie, you'll find many exciting ideas from which to choose. The irresistible novelty of these works will open your mind to things you might never have imagined. To encourage you along the way, you'll read inspiring and revealing thoughts from the artists about their creative experiences.

Maybe you're a bookmaker who is ready to venture beyond the standard format of the 12 x 12 page. For convenience, we've adopted the term substrate, often used by artists, which refers to the structure that supports a piece of artwork, such as a canvas or a particular kind of paper. For our purposes, it describes the underpinnings of a scrapbook ranging from a box holding loose paper pages to a handmade book; from a purchased or recycled book to a folding book made out of polymer clay "pages"—in other words, any structure that serves to hold journal components.

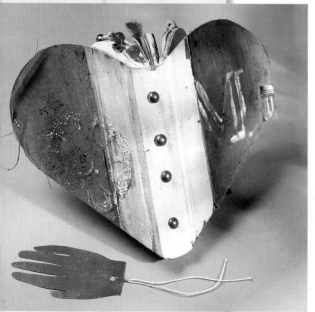

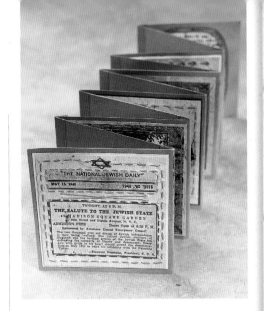

But being adventuresome doesn't mean you have to leave the world of tradition behind. Far from it! The focus of each book is grounded in the traditional meaning of journaling, because every book documents something personal—a memory, a moment, an event or series of events, or some snippets of ordinary life.

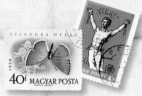

You'll put your unique spin on things, while expanding your vision with "new" materials and concepts. And what about all those paper-crafting supplies you already have on hand? You'll be impressed by the innovative ways you can use them.

It goes without saying that photos will play a major role in your adventurous storytelling. We'll show you how to make your pages

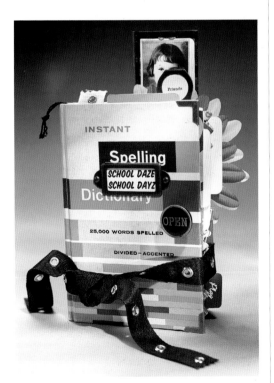

visually compelling while also effectively communicating your theme. To decorate the pages further, you can use any media you wish, such as artist's paints or pastels.

You'll use loads of interesting papers, memorabilia, ephemera, and embellishments.

Unlike what we think of as some traditional scrapbooks, these books are not necessarily precious, so you won't have to worry about wearing out their pages as you share them with friends. They might find their way into your handbag, or they might be displayed upright on your dining room table. Make them more interactive by adding pop-ups, pockets, slide-out tags, and other moveable parts.

So prepare for blastoff as you dip into the well of creativity that the talented artists in this book offer to you. If you're ready to take the trip, the onset of your adventure is only a page away.

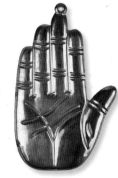

"I love the idea of alternative substrates for journals because I can display the finished project more easily than a traditional scrapbook, inviting interaction from viewers."

—STEPHANIE JONES RUBIANO

"I like using alternative substrates and have been doing this since I began journaling three years ago in my biology lab book! Old ceiling tins, record albums, and vintage book covers are just a few examples of things I've used to make scrapbooking creations."

—SARAH FISHBURN

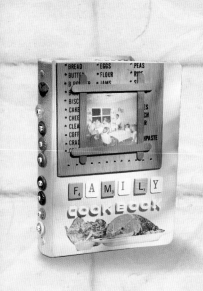

> "I am a natural-born collector of stuff, but not just any stuff—it has to be special. Sometimes I don't even know what it is, it's just cool, and I like it!"
>
> —MARY LAWLER

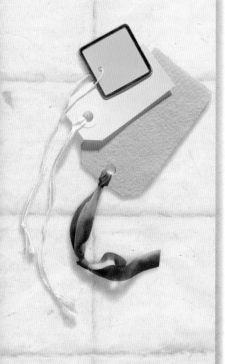

BECOMING AN ADVENTUROUS STORYTELLER

You'll find that many of the materials and tools you need to venture outside of the box are already in your scrapbooking arsenal. Use them in new ways, and you will find yourself on a unique and adventurous journey.

Creativity does not spell difficulty. It simply means being open to new possibilities. In this opening chapter you'll discover more than the basics. You'll begin to think about things in a new way and open your eyes to a new world of both materials and ideas.

SUPPLIES AND TOOLS

Less is not necessarily more in the scrapbooking world, and you'll discover that accumulating some appealing materials feeds your creative verve. However, acquiring this "stuff" doesn't mean you have to spend a fortune.

Just be selective and resourceful. There are some basic supplies and tools that will serve you well, and you can find other things for practically nothing.

Transforming the Ordinary: Unusual Supplies

Scavenging for fabrics, old books, magazines, found objects, and things that you might think otherwise useless can become a healthy obsession for an adventurous scrapbooker. In fact, it's a natural fit. This process is often the beginning of a wonderful idea.

So next time you find yourself peering into your trash can, count yourself among the world's creative people—artists have done it for years. Or take a trip to any thrift shop, hardware store, or flea market, and you'll begin to discover things to recontextualize and use in your work.

For just pennies, you can fill up boxes with things from which you can readily select when inspiration strikes. If the "something" you find fascinates you, don't worry about how silly or mundane it might seem to somebody else, just grab it and go! Don't contemplate its future, which will only deaden your enthusiasm.

To give you some actual examples of this, Erikia Ghumm bought an old metal recipe box at a thrift store one day to add to an already brimming collection. She really didn't need it, but she found it irresistible, which was all she needed to know. Later she transformed it into the festive holiday piece shown on page 80. Terry Taylor bought a children's board book on sale simply because he liked its shape. It sat in his workroom for a long time before he was asked to create a mixed-media journal for this publication—and voilà!—it now has a new use as a book about a lifetime of houses (see page 22). To add to this, he unearthed the café curtains pictured in an old photo, and used scraps of them in his book to make it more real. Many of the ideas for books you'll see in the pages that follow were sparked by the influence of a long-hoarded item.

The Usual Suspects: Commonly Used Supplies

In the world of paper crafting, there are some commonly used supplies that practically everyone has on hand. You probably already have many of these materials, since some are almost essentials. Add to these some art media, and you'll have more ways to express your imagination.

PAPERS

Choose papers that fit the purpose of your project. If you're making an heirloom piece, you'll need to use archival papers, but informal bookmaking doesn't require them, so you have a lot more choices. For instance, if you're making a mini-album to tote around and show your friends (a piece "of the moment"), use whatever you like. Here's a list of some commonly used scrapbooking papers and their potential uses:

■ Cardstock: This is a sturdy paper that is often used for backgrounds, framing images, and decorative accents. If you're making your own book, cardstock is a standard choice for pages.

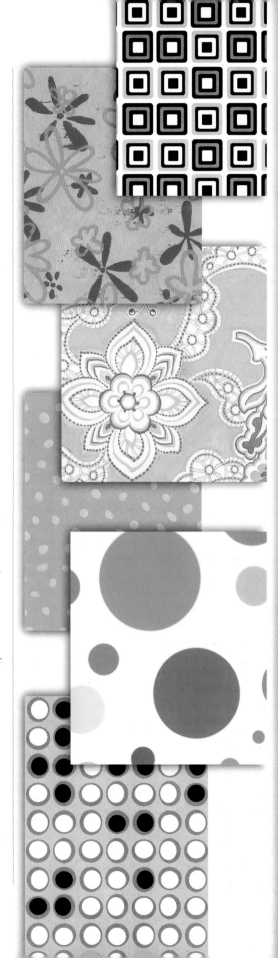

"I believe that inspiration is absolutely everywhere and in everything. Artists have always had an appreciation for the little things. Collage and mixed media artists have a genuine love for life's castoffs and for elevating the mundane. A candy wrapper found on the sidewalk can become the focal point for an entire piece! As scrapbooking evolves and moves further away from the cookie cutter aspect, every journaler's vision becomes broader, giving each of us more and more room for creativity."

—LINDA WARLYN

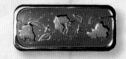

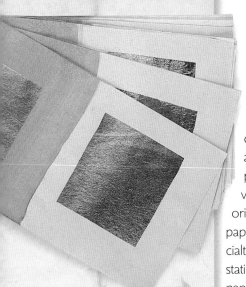

■ **Patterned paper:** This category includes just about every imaginable pattern and design. Many choices are available at craft supply and paper-crafting stores, but venture outside of that orb for original ideas. What about artist's papers, gift wraps from party specialty stores, handsome papers from stationary stores, and handmade papers from specialty stores?

■ **Vellum:** Modeled after the translucent pages made of animal skins from the olden days, these popular papers now come in a wide range of colors. Most people use these papers for layering or journaling. Laser-printer-friendly vellum is a great option for adding computer-generated text to your journal.

■ **Found papers:** Old magazines, newspapers, books, greeting cards, and even commercial wrappings have always been the papers of choice for collage artists. Incorporate them into your scrapbooks, and they will give your work an authentic touch. Plus, it's really fun to think of such items in a new way. Before you know it, you won't be reading the back of your cereal box, you'll be cutting it up and using it in your mixed-media journal!

■ **Chipboard:** This thin and durable cardboard is used to make book covers. You can find it at craft and art stores.

> "I encourage you to think outside the box and not limit yourself to materials that come from paper supply stores. Use watercolor or charcoal papers instead of standard scrapbooking papers. Draw, paint, and collage on this paper… or have one of your children do it."
>
> **—KAREN TIMM**

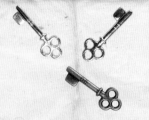

BOOKMAKING "STUFF"

The following terms that define categories of materials allow you to make your work highly individual.

■ **Memorabilia:** These are things connected to events, culture, or entertainment—such as travel brochures and maps, stamps, postcards, tickets to a play, sporting event posters, and so forth. In other words, all those accumulated things in a drawer that you've placed there in hopes of not losing your memory of a particular event.

■ **Ephemera:** Ephemera is simply defined as printed matter of passing importance, such as magazines and newspapers. There are some similarities between memorabilia and ephemera. Think of ephemera as the matriculations of your daily life—seemingly mundane, but not necessarily so when placed in the right context. Found papers (see above) are ephemera.

■ **Embellishments:** This is another fondly used bookmaking term that simply means anything you use to "dress up" a page once you've established its major components. Embellishments are the decorative additions such as ribbons, bows, charms, silk flowers, beads, buttons, colored eyelets, and all of those beloved

paper crafting dodads . . . the cherries on the whipped cream. Depending on your personality and taste, you might opt for a minimal amount of this decoration or go for over-the-top showy embellishment.

ART SUPPLIES

Art supplies hold a special place in every creative person's heart. Go to any art store, and you'll get fired up with inspiration. You can use these materials to add touches of color, shading, detail, and even creative backgrounds to your book pages. Try out anything that interests you.

■ Colored pencils: You are more than familiar with these! Use them to fill in stamped images, write words, make small drawings, or do shading.

■ Chalk and oil pastels: Experiment with both of these to discover the different effects you can achieve. The array of colors available is virtually unlimited, especially if you blend this medium. Chalk pastels are dry, while oil pastels are creamy. Spray a fixative over chalk pastels to keep them from smearing.

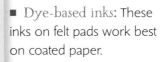

■ Acrylic paints: These paints can be applied to anything. Not only can you do the usual things with them, such as paint backgrounds and simple images, but you can also use them to color small objects. For instance, change the color of a found object, such as a coin or key.

■ Watercolors: Washes of watercolor can be used to create beautiful, delicate backgrounds, and they can even be applied

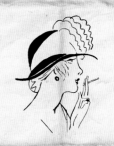

over permanent hand lettering to create a veil. Use them to fill in simple shapes drawn with a permanent ink marker.

STAMPING SUPPLIES

Journal pages can be enlivened with ready-made images that can be replicated or changed by switching inks or even the amount of pressure you apply to the stamp.

■ Dye-based inks: These inks on felt pads work best on coated paper.

■ Pigment inks: These thicker inks on foam pads are opaque and slow to dry. They are more resistant to fading and work well on absorbent, uncoated paper such as card stock. Because of their thickness, they're the ink of choice for embossing.

■ Embossing powders: Sprinkle these on top of pigment inks and dry them with a heat gun to create a tactile, embossed look.

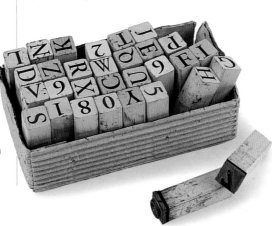

"Unless it's a piece or page that I've visualized in my mind's eye in its entirety, I have a kind of intuitive feeling about when a particular piece is finished. Because I belong to the 'more is more' camp of artists, I'll often add just one more thing until I'm satisfied that the filled space holds more interest than the empty."

—SARAH FISHBURN

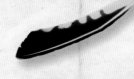

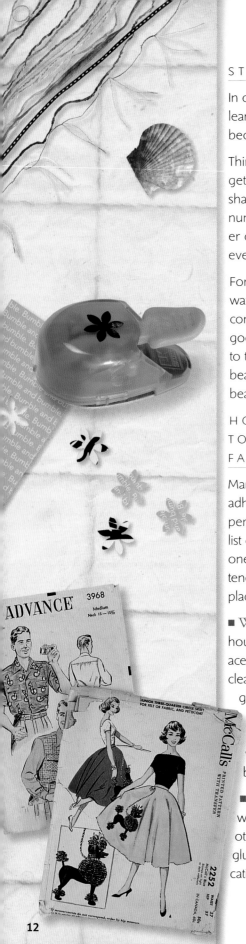

STITCHING SUPPLIES

In case you haven't noticed, what you learned in home economics class has become a craze for paper artists of all types.

Think of thread as a medium, and you'll get the idea. You can outline, draw, and shade with it. It comes in an awesome number of colors. Hand-stitching is another option if you want your pages to look even more personal.

For stitching by hand, embroidery floss or waxed linen are good choices, and they come in many colors. Waxed linen is also a good material for sewing simple signatures to the spine of a handmade book. Use beading thread if you wish to add tiny beads to your pages.

HOLDING THINGS TOGETHER: ADHESIVES AND FASTENERS

Many options are available in the world of adhesives. Bookmakers develop their own personal preferences, and what follows is a list of a few of the most commonly used ones. Also mentioned in this section are fasteners, which are used to hold things in place and to decorate pages.

- **White craft glue (PVA):** This is common household glue. PVA stands for polyvinyl acetate. It's permanent, holds well, and dries clear. If you use a brush to spread this glue into a thin layer on the back of a piece of paper, and then use a brayer to press it onto the page, there will be less chance of the applied piece buckling.

- **Glue stick:** This glue applicator works well for adhering smaller bits of paper or other material to a scrapbook page. This glue is best suited for paper-to-paper applications. Some glue sticks are permanent;

others are not and allow you to reposition things. In general, they are less susceptible to wrinkling than more fluid glues are.

- **Glue pen:** If you're working with tiny pieces of material, try a glue pen. You can trace a small amount of glue onto a very specific area.

- **Tacky glue:** This thick glue also dries clear and works well for holding embellishments on a page.

- **Spray adhesive:** This adhesive works well for covering larger areas, and it won't buckle. You can pull the piece off of the page and reapply it without leaving a stain. Cover your work surface when using it to prevent overspray. Remove fumes by always ventilating your workspace when using this adhesive.

- **Cyanoacrylate glues:** This is smply the long name for "super" or "crazy" glue, which will give you an extremely strong and quick bond. It works well for attaching objects to a cover or page.

- **Artist's acrylic medium:** This medium is thinner than craft glue and can be applied with a paintbrush. You can also paint it on as a final layer.

- **Double-sided tape:** This transparent tape can be cut to any length, and it works well for adhering paper and photos without having to worry about buckling.

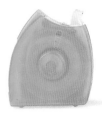

- **Pop-up dots and foam tape:** These raised adhesive materials allow you to elevate an item slightly off of the page.

- **Tapes:** You can use masking tape, colored artist's tape, or even electrical tape to hold things to the page. It all depends on the look and feel you want to create on the page.

- **Photo corners:** These are those nice old-fashioned corners that were often used in traditional scrapbooks to hold photos. They add a nostalgic touch to your pages.

- **Sticker machine with adhesive sheets:** This popular machine applies an even layer of adhesive to an entire surface.

- **Eyelets and brads:** These small fasteners are inserted into punched holes in pages and other materials. Both eyelets and brads add a finished touch to the page and come in a range of colors. They also come in a variety of sizes and work well for holding multiple layers to a page.

- **Office supplies:** Experiment with using staples or paper clips to hold things in place if you want to create an informal look.

Tools

You don't need many tools for scrapbooking. Below are things that are often used, but all you really need to begin a mixed-media journal is a pair of scissors, a craft knife, and a cutting mat.

- **Scissors/craft knife:** You'll perpetually use these tools to cut, snip, and trim. A craft knife allows you to create a cleaner, more precise edge, such as when you are cutting windows and small shapes. Always use a fresh blade.

- **Cutting mat:** Protect your work surface with a self-healing cutting mat.

- **Rubber stamps:** Stamps provide you with a huge range of imagery and text possibilities. Buying a whole alphabet in a font that you like is a great investment for creating wording.

- **Awl:** An awl is a small pointed tool that is used to punch small holes in paper for the purpose of hand-stitching. Awls are also used to make holes in signatures for the purpose of binding them into a handmade book.

- **Bone folder:** This bookbinding tool is used to score and neatly fold paper. It is used to fold the pages of a handmade book.

- **Brayer:** Use this roller to remove bubbles under paper and prevent it from lifting in the future. Do this right after you've adhered the paper to the page.

- **Hole and shaped punches:** A traditional round hole punch from an office supply store can be used to punch holes for binding a handmade book or for creating small decorative circles. A circle cutter is a tool that can be adjusted to punch circles in a range of diameters. Square punches work well for cutting windows. Besides geometric punches, you'll find a wide variety of shaped punches in the scrapbooking section of a craft store.

- **Eyelet-setting tools:** This set is composed of a mat to protect your work surface, a hole punch made for punching an eyelet-sized hole, an eyelet setter for securing the eyelet, and a small hammer for applying force to the setter.

- **Computer and printer:** Use your computer to generate text in various fonts, to alter images in a photo-editing program, or to transport your digital images to the printing stage.

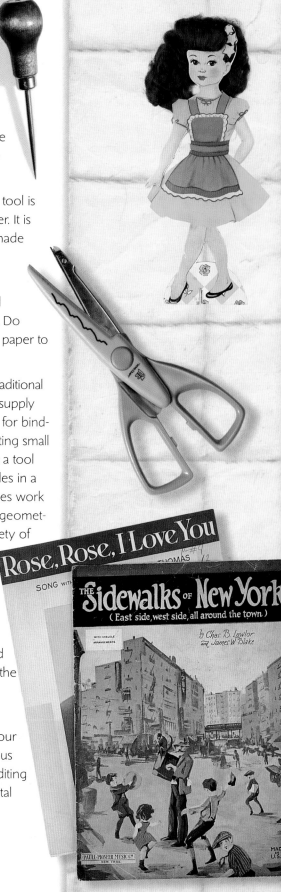

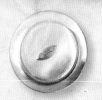

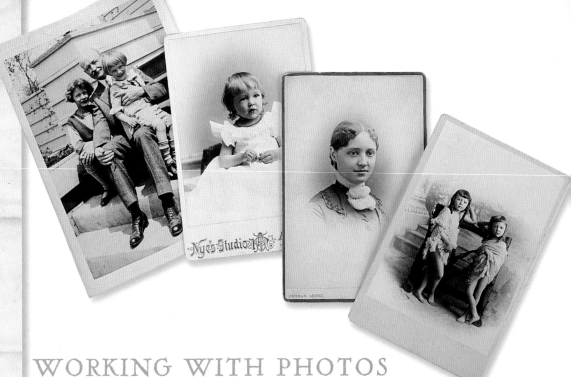

"Sometimes my artwork is an effective soul-searching tool. It's a place where I can go and work through life happenings, both good and bad. I don't always want people to get exactly what a page is saying; but if the elements pull together and express what I want to say, I'm happy with the end result."

—STEPHANIE MCATEE

WORKING WITH PHOTOS

Back in the olden days, we mounted photos in albums for safekeeping with the help of those nifty photo corners that held fast for a couple of years before they began slowly falling off the pages. The photos were occasionally removed to scrutinize a detail before carefully returning them to their placeholders.

In one of our old family albums, my older sister wrote short captions underneath our traditional deckle-edged photos. "Watch out kitty!" she scrawled underneath a picture of me gleefully grabbing a distressed looking tabby by the neck. Those photos are so precious to all of us now as we laugh and look back at what seemed to be a much more innocent time.

Today, personal bookmaking has evolved into an art as well as a way of organizing and remembering things. We duplicate photos and keep the original film or digital files stored away and undamaged while we freely experiment with images. Instead of the actual photos, it is the memories and surrounding thoughts that are precious, and the image is simply a storytelling component. In other words,

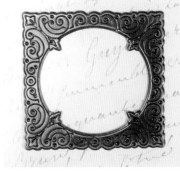

photos are vehicles for feelings and thoughts that take us back to a certain place. Moments captured photographically are enhanced by any number of other materials that lend them highly personal meaning.

Without the invention of the photocopying machine, the computer, and the digital camera, we might still be mounting original images on pages. Today's journalers have lots of choices when it comes to photos, and they usually have certain preferences. Because you can easily duplicate

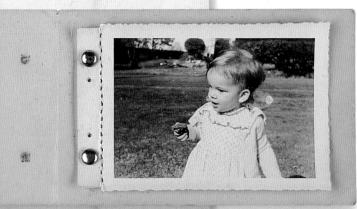

photos from the original negatives or output them digitally, some artists still prefer to use what resembles an "original" photo. If you are using old photos, you can scan the photos and print them onto photo paper to achieve the look of an original.

Using a color photocopier to copy originals is another great option. Some scrapbookers prefer to take things a step further and alter photos in a computer photo-editing program. The photographic possibilities are very expansive, and working with a stack of nonprecious, duplicate photos can be freeing. Why not experiment? You'll have more latitude in telling your story, and more room to be an artist. You might want to reinvent history a bit and put your own spin on it.

You can also transfer photos directly onto paper or fabric. Use inkjet transfer paper with an inkjet printer or a simple blender pen that contains the transfer solvent called xylene. To transfer an image with a blender pen, choose a high-contrast image and photocopy it in reverse so it will appear correctly after it has been transferred. Saturate the entire image with the pen, place it facedown on the transfer paper or fabric, and rub the back of the image with a bone folder or spoon. Lift up a corner to check your progress. Add more solvent if you aren't satisfied with the results. You can add color to this transferred image with art media such as colored pencils or paints.

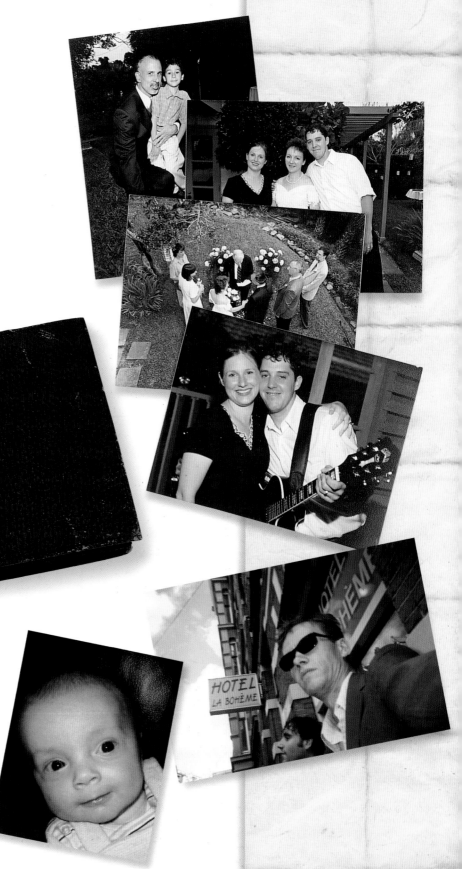

PLANNING AND IMPROVISING

Many of the artists featured in this book will tell you that they don't characteristically plan their work. They begin with a very general concept and then "let the spirit move them." Terry Taylor calls this "puttering," while Luann Udell likens herself to a "magpie" picking through her hoard of shiny treasures. Claudine Helmuth is another self-described improviser, noting that her best

adventurous, it's almost impossible to plan every detail, and that's what keeps the work so fresh. It's also what makes it fun.

If you're not accustomed to cutting loose in this way, try thinking about only the key components of your journal, keeping it simple. For instance, if you have a main photo around which your theme revolves (such as an irresistible picture of Aunt Hilda), then spin your ideas off that image. Think of words, stories, and items you associate with this person. Before you know it, you'll have many ideas. Look through papers, fabrics, and embellishments to accompany the image in your mind. When you do this, you've already "begun" your piece, and you haven't even gotten out your glue stick yet!

Assemble your items on your worktable, and muse for a while as you move things around. "Nah . . . that shade of blue really doesn't work with the image . . . but, hey, this green really sings! And wouldn't it be a hoot to have a swatch of fabric that reminds me of the apron my aunt wore?" Pretty soon you'll be playing with all sorts

> "I love 'good for the soul' work…simply creating what I feel without boundaries."
> —**STEPHANIE McATTEE**

work emerges when she allows the process to take her in the most creative direction possible.

You might find that just the right amount of planning will lend you the direction you need without squelching new ideas that might emerge while you're working. If you really intend to be

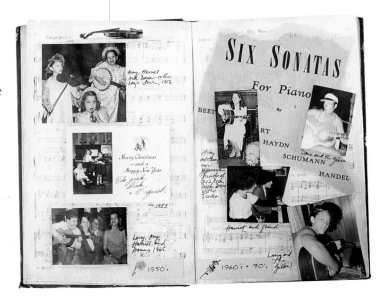

16

of items that lead you to other ideas. Then you might have to decide what to keep and what not to use.

Begin with very simple pages and work up to more elaborate ones. Don't overdo it, or the page might become so busy that you lose your point of emphasis. Be selective. As you work, always keep in mind your theme as well as points of visual emphasis. If a page becomes confusing, remove some items and look at it again so you can get some clarity. As in collage, you can play around with various pieces of paper, photos, and other items to gain a real sense of how they will look before attaching them.

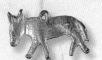

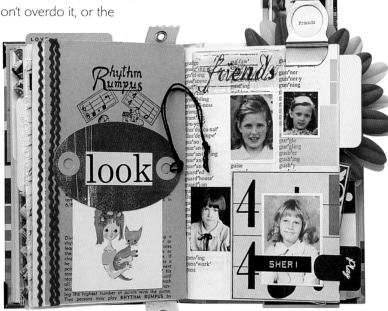

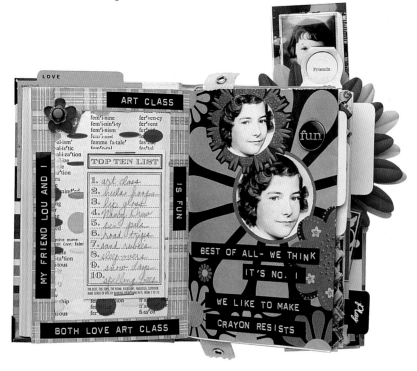

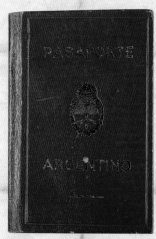

"Often I'll plan an entire composition in my head, but sometimes I'll give myself a challenge to grab whatever is in front of me and turn it into a workable piece... When I work on a particular book, I might want it to sparkle with brilliant color while retaining an element of mystery, leaving a bit of untold story to be guessed at, along with the unanswered question: 'What happens next?'"

—SARAH FISHBURN

how to really unleash your creative potential? Before you begin your story, ponder some of these suggestions and musings. To be adventurous in your scrapbooking, all you really have to do is try new things. With this type of journaling, "thinking outside of the box" might simply mean putting your pages into a box!

■ Create books with themes that really excite you. If you're not hearing a distinct "yes!" about an idea, you're probably not going to enjoy making the piece. In turn, the work may end up looking forced.

■ Keep a stockpile of inspiring supplies and embellishments on hand so you can simply pick and choose while you work. You might already have just the right swatch of vintage fabric to go with a particular photo when you need it.

■ Use your arsenal of materials as inspiration. Thumb through papers, photos, and embellishments, and allow your imagination to lead you.

■ Think of each page as an adventure and a story in itself.

■ Invite and embrace the unexpected rather than running away from it. If you accidentally spill some paint, consider the idea that it might work with your design.

■ Bend the rules.

■ Stay relaxed and have fun. Take breaks when you get frustrated, then come back with a fresh perspective.

■ Add embellishments to your page that support your theme or evoke emotions.

■ Experiment until you instinctively find the right solution to a design question. The best decisions couple instinct with experience.

■ Always choose materials that make your heart sing. Don't feel obligated to "use up" a box of chalks that somebody brought you back from Italy, no mater how exotic they might seem! Move on to find materials that excite you.

■ Be willing to change your mind. Begin with a concept, but don't let that hold you back as you create the piece. If it isn't working, try something else.

■ Begin with the big picture and then elaborate on the details, without losing yourself in them. This larger view is what holds the piece together visually.

■ Don't be intimidated by the blank page; just begin. If that empty page is driving you

---

"I find it helpful to 'center' the project on something in my heart. Trying to figure out what other people will think is cool or wonderful sends me into a tizzy! But making something that pleases ME almost always turns out well."

—**LUANN UDELL**

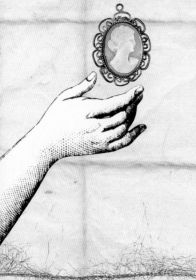

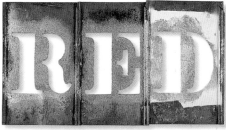

RED

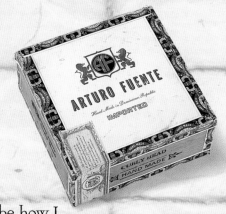

nuts and keeping you stuck, simply "mess it up." You can always paint over it, cover it up, or alter it in some way. Don't take the process too seriously.

■ Inspiration is everywhere, if you just take the time to notice it. Attune yourself to contemplation of the visual, and you'll never lack for ideas.

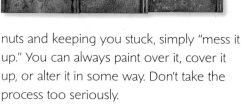

"I can't describe how I recognize when a piece is complete…it just is. Sometimes I have to let it sit for a while when it isn't working and return to it later with fresh eyes."

—STEPHANIE RUBIANO

"As eternal hunters and gatherers, we have a large stash of objects on hand to choose from for any given piece we create."

—LINDA AND OPIE O'BRIEN

"My inspiration for each project is different. Sometimes it's a line from a book, movie, poem, or song…or a particular photo. Other times I am inspired by the accidental way bits and pieces fall onto my worktable, layered on top of one another…"

—SARAH FISHBURN

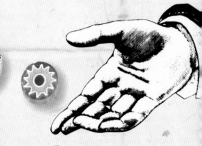

"I once based an entire collage on the colors and patterns of a carpet in a hotel lobby. When I get excited about things like that, my friends often quietly walk away. And yes…I even look through trash!"

—MARY LAWLER

THE PROJECTS

Choose from 30 projects made by some of today's most noted handmade book designers. The broad range of projects will whet your appetite for making your own adventurous journal. Ranging from fun and kitschy to nostalgic and heartfelt, these works express the maker's very personal thoughts and feelings. You'll find your own voice for each book you create by drawing inspiration from this amazing collection.

The variety of substrates used shows you just how imaginative you can get. Whether you choose to use an old book befitting your theme, a box that is just the right size and shape for your pages, recycled CDs or a mail order catalogue that you would normally throw away—you'll be surprised at what you can transform into work that truly approaches art.

Study the projects to gain ideas and learn about techniques. The instructions are meant to guide you into understanding what each artist did and why they made certain choices. The quotes written by the artists provide you with a personal look at their thoughts about the books.

You'll make your own unique interpretations from these projects, and you might even improve upon the original concept. Stay open to possibilities that you find interesting. Hey, we can't wait to see what you come up with!

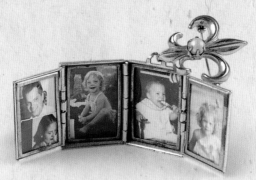

REMEMBER...

Almost every journal is based on a personal
collection of remembrances. The projects shown in this
section reflect on lives well lived, the coming and going of
events. Begin by collecting ephemera and photos from
those you love and allow a theme to emerge.

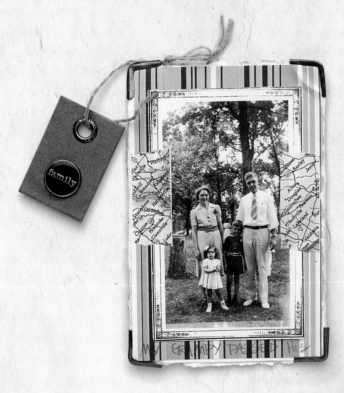

THIS IS THE FIRST HOUSE...   ARTIST: TERRY TAYLOR

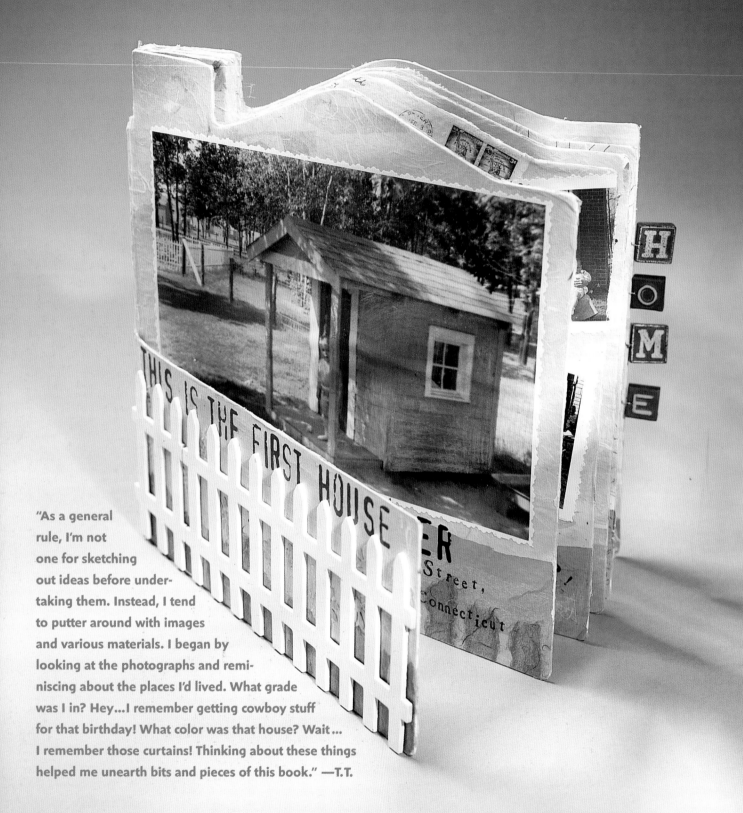

"As a general rule, I'm not one for sketching out ideas before undertaking them. Instead, I tend to putter around with images and various materials. I began by looking at the photographs and reminiscing about the places I'd lived. What grade was I in? Hey...I remember getting cowboy stuff for that birthday! What color was that house? Wait... I remember those curtains! Thinking about these things helped me unearth bits and pieces of this book." —T.T.

Terry had been squirreling away boxes of vintage family photos for several years. When asked to make an "adventurous" yet personal journal, he was instantly attracted to a children's board book with a house shape. The heavy pages serve as a perfect substrate for holding collaged photos and papers that inventively document the many houses of his life.

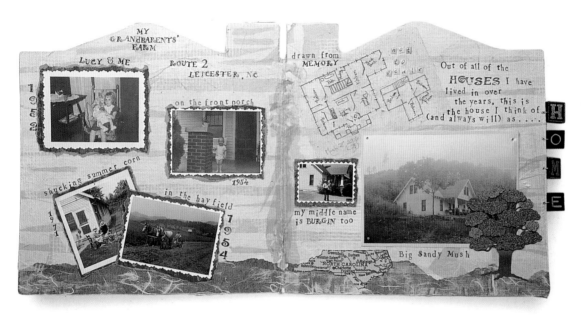

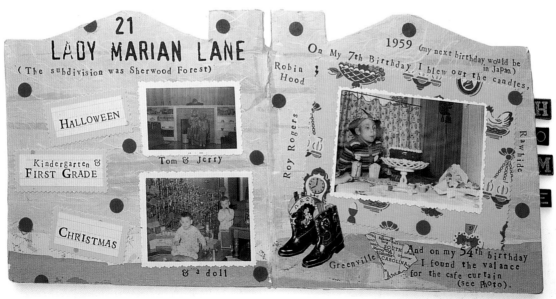

BOOK AND PAGES

- Children's board book
- Gesso or white acrylic paint
- Colored tissue, thin white Oriental, decorative, and vintage papers
- Acrylic medium
- Photocopies of vintage photographs
- Vintage ephemera such as fabric swatches, maps, and gameboard letters
- Wire

TOOLS

- Sanding sponge
- Paintbrush
- Craft knife
- Decorative-edged scissors
- Sticker machine
- Lettering stencils and rubberstamps
- Colored pencils and pens
- Hole punch
- Hand drill

1. Lightly sand the covers and pages of the book. After sanding, paint the pages with at least one coat of gesso or white acrylic paint to prevent buckling. Let one side of the pages dry thoroughly before you paint the other side.

2. Tear colored tissue papers into strips, feathering the edges and creating a soft look. Brush a coat of acrylic medium onto a small area before laying down the strips, beginning at the bottom of each page. Overlap the strips and apply more medium as needed to create your background. To soften the colors and create subtle variation, Terry layered white Oriental papers on top of the ground in various places.

3. Cut out the photocopies of your photos. Terry used deckle-edged scissors to give them a true vintage photo look.

4. Use a sticker machine with adhesive sheets or another adhesive of your choice to apply the photos. To "frame" the photos, layer decorative papers underneath each one.

5. Add vintage ephemera to your pages, such as maps of places, pictures of clothing from your era, bits of vintage fabric, or found objects. Stamp words onto your pages with lettering stamps to create your commentary.

6. As a finishing touch, Terry attached drilled gameboard letters to the side of the book with bits of wire fitted through the holes.

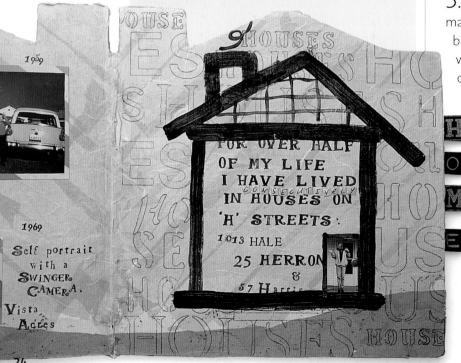

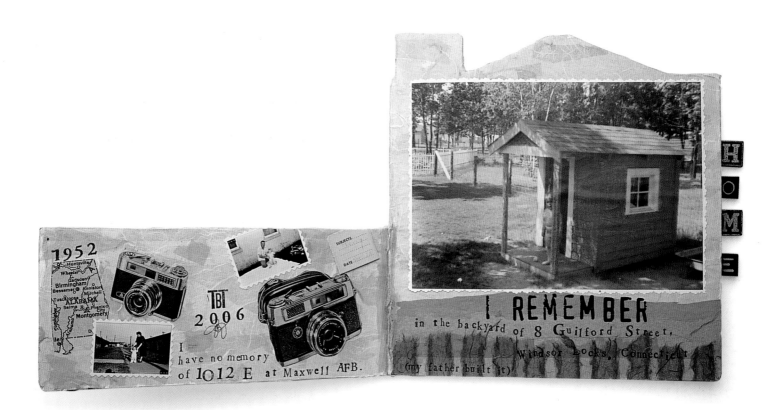

1952

I have no memory of 1012 E at Maxwell AFB.

TBT 2006

I REMEMBER

in the backyard of 8 Guilford Street,

Windsor Locks, Connecticut

(my father built it)

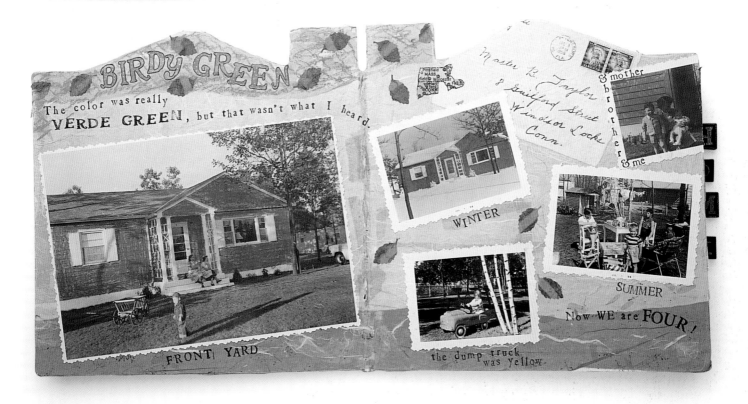

BIRDY GREEN

The color was really VERDE GREEN, but that wasn't what I heard

Master B. Taylor
8 Guilford Street
Windsor Locks
Conn.

mother
brother & me

FRONT YARD

WINTER

the dump truck was yellow

SUMMER

Now WE are FOUR!

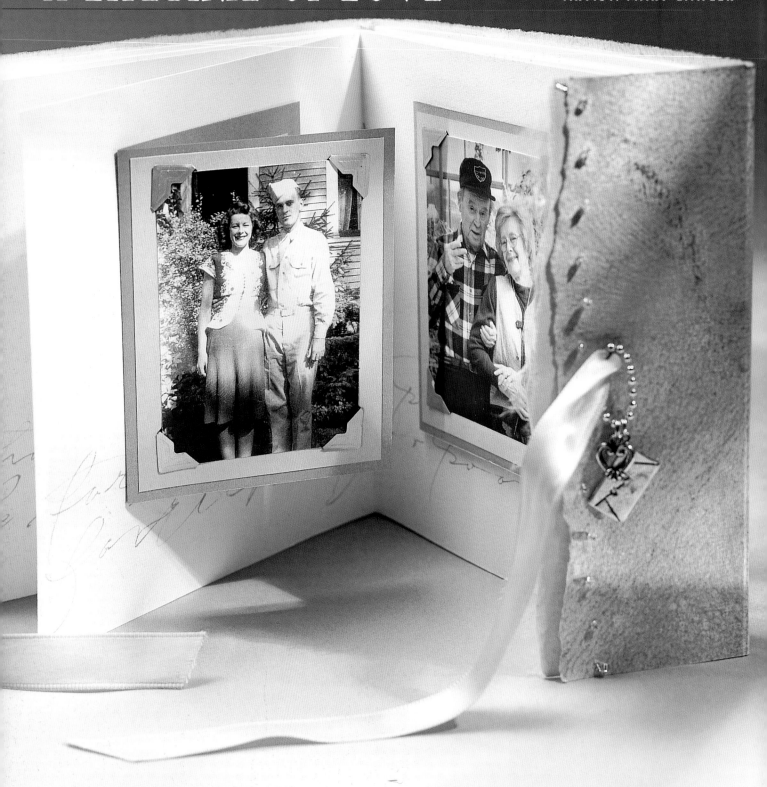

On each spread of this simple handmade book, the artist tenderly juxtaposes past and recent photos of her parents. Each photo is mounted on a "card," so the typed journaling inside doesn't interfere with the clean look of the spreads. Artistically scripted words serve as background designs. An elegant cover dignifies the precious content of the book.

BOOK

- Simple handmade book with two signatures
- Metallic powders (available through art or craft suppliers)
- Flour paste
- Text-weight artist's paper
- Japanese lace paper
- Linen binding thread
- Seed beads
- Silver embroidery thread
- Dry sheet adhesive
- Small eyelets, ribbon, and charms

PAGES

- Photocopies of photos
- Metallic and opalescent papers for photo backgrounds and text
- Silver self-adhesive photo corners

TOOLS

- Natural sponges
- Silver gel and clear glitter pens
- Craft knife
- Bone folder
- Computer and printer
- Small eyelets, eyelet setter, and small hammer

"When my parents passed away, only months apart, they left my family with many wonderful memories about their lives. Later, we found boxes and albums filled with pictures. We knew the stories of the more recent ones, but the earlier black-and-white photos were a mystery. Except for a few words or a date here and there, we were left to imagine our own stories." —M.L.

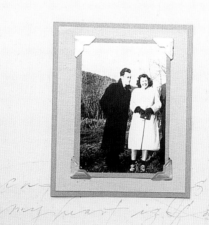
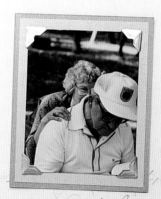

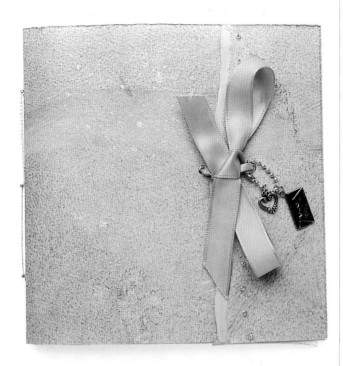

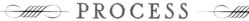
1. Mary chose to use hand-decorated paste paper for the folded cover of her book. This paste paper is fairly simple to make. Begin by mixing various metallic powders in flour paste to create a shade that you like. (She mixed gray metallic powder with bits of silver, black, and rose metallic powders).

2. Apply the paste, one side at a time, to a piece of text-weight artist's paper, and spread it out with natural sponges and your fingers. You can also use combs, stamps, or other tools to create texture. There's no right or wrong way to do this. After you've finished one side, allow it to dry, and then decorate the other side so the inside of your cover will also look pretty.

3. Cut the cover paper to two and a half times the width of the front of your finished book, so you can overlap the cover in the front to form a closure. Trim a piece of lace paper to fit inside the cover, allowing a bit of extra width.

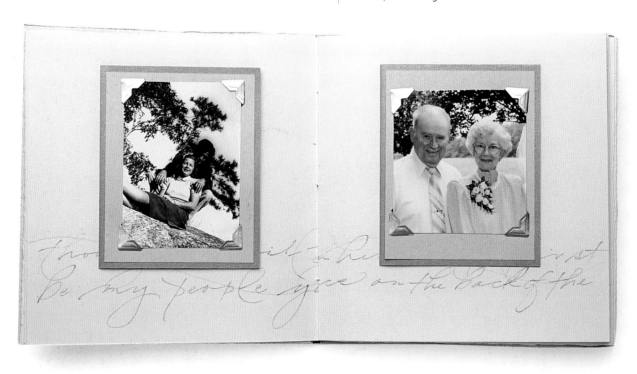

4. Cut the inside book pages from text-weight artist's paper as well. (Mary used two interior signatures of 16 pages each.)

5. Because Mary is a calligrapher, she created the bottom border of each page spread with words from love poems and wedding vows written freely with silver gel and clear glitter pens. It's much easier to do this before the pages are folded and sewn together. Because the calligraphy is semi-abstract, it doesn't matter whether the words read clearly all the way across the spread.

6. To form the book, sew the two interior signatures with linen binding thread. Sew each one to the exposed spine of the cover with embroidery thread. Tear the edge of the front flap, and sew a single flowing line of glass beads along the edge with the embroidery thread, hiding the thread on the backside of the flap.

7. To create a layered look along the edge of the flap, tear a piece of blank artist's paper to slide underneath it, exposing the edges of the paper and concealing your sewing. Tear the interior lace paper so a bit of it shows as well. Tack the edges of these inside papers down with dry sheet adhesive.

8. Use the hammer and eyelet punch to punch a hole in the flap and a corresponding hole in the cover. Insert small eyelets to reinforce the openings for the ribbon. Thread the ribbon inside the flap, behind the lace paper inside the cover, and out the hole in the front of the cover on the other side. To finish the cover, Mary sewed two silver charms on a chain to the ribbon.

9. Cut folded paper "cards" to fit on each page and layer the fronts of them with papers before attaching your photos with self-adhesive photo corners. Inside each card, use dry sheet adhesive to attach computer-generated journaling printed on pretty paper.

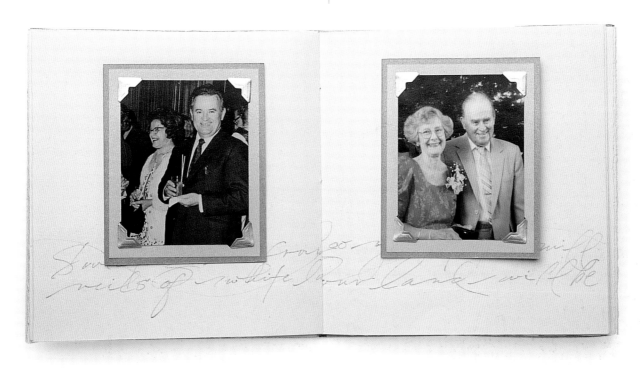

MY GRANDMOTHER'S LONG LIFE

ARTIST: CAROL MCGOOGAN

"This book is in memory of my grandmother, Loretta Holzbach Carney, who I loved and admired very much. She had a long and interesting life, full of both joy and hardship. My grandmother was a beautiful woman, both inside and out. I wanted to preserve bits of the story of her life, and I love the texture and feel of fabric. Softness was what I wanted to portray when I looked at the old photos, so fabric with photo transfers made the perfect substrate for my theme." —C.M.

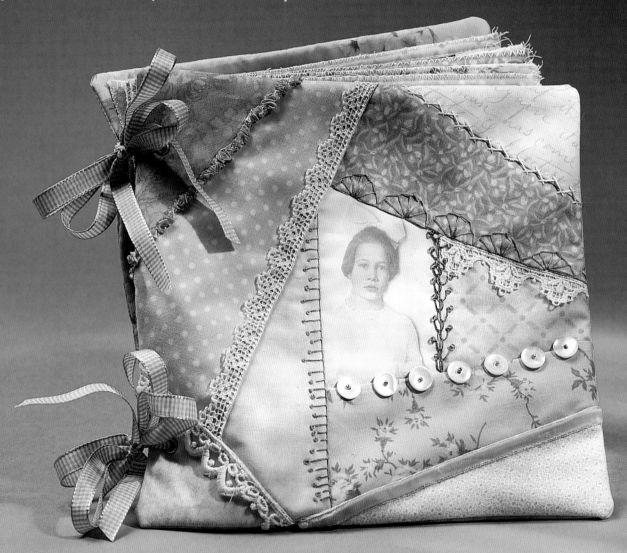

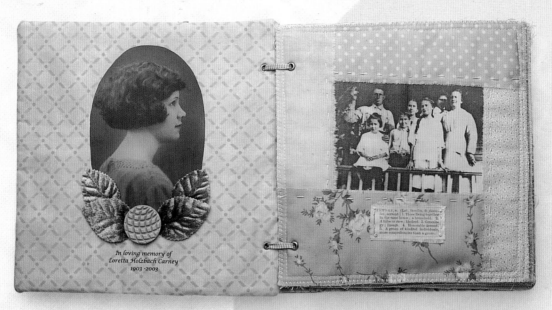

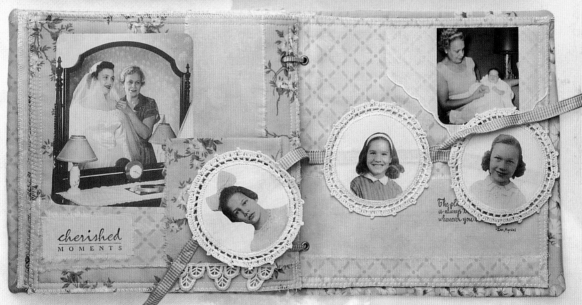

This fabric book celebrating the artist's grandmother presents a visual story of her long life. It is made with a combination of machine stitching, handstitching, and quilting. The photos are printed or transferred onto fabric; the text is printed or stamped onto the fabric; and then the fabric is embellished with ribbons, buttons, embroidery, and beads.

BOOK AND PAGES

- Assorted printed fabrics for page backgrounds and embellishments
- Solid-colored fabric (such as muslin) for transfers
- Sewing thread
- Embroidery floss for handstitching
- Embellishments: trims, ribbons, buttons, beads, small frames, and vintage handwork
- Low-loft cotton quilt batting
- Fabric sheets with paper backing, fabric sheets with fusible backing, and iron–on transfer paper for ink-jet printers (available at larger fabric stores)
- Fusible webbing for attaching images
- Tacky glue for attaching embellishments
- Preprinted twill tape and found-fabric text (such as printing on fabric selvages)
- Alphabet stamps and permanent-ink stamp pad, or rub-on letters
- Eyelets

TOOLS

- Sewing machine
- Embroidery needle
- Computer, scanner, photo-editing program, and ink-jet printer
- Clothes iron
- Fabric scissors
- 8-inch square quilt ruler
- Erasable fabric marking pencil
- Japanese screw punch
- Eyelet setter and hammer

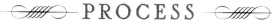

PROCESS

1. Carol wanted to make the cover of this book resemble a crazy quilt. She transferred a central photo to a 9-inch square piece of muslin using iron-on photo transfer paper (see step 4). She sewed random-sized pieces of printed fabric around the image, working out in a spiral direction. Once pieced, she added embellishments (such as tacked lace, embroidery, and ribbons) along each of the seams. Then she completed her design on the inside cover page.

2. When you've finished the front cover pieces, place the right sides of the fabric pieces together. Add a layer of quilt batting on top, pin, and stitch around the edges to create an 8-inch square when you turn the piece. Hand-stitch the opening closed. Create a back cover by stitching and turning two fabric pieces of the same size.

3. To make the pages, begin by cutting or tearing fabric into 9-inch squares to serve as backgrounds. When transferring an image directly onto a page, you can use a solid fabric as the background so the pattern doesn't interfere with the image. If you wish to use a patterned background behind an image, photocopy or print the photos and images onto sheets of fabric made for ink-jet printers (see step 4 for more information). If your photos are old or photocopies of an original, you can use a computer photo-editing program to enhance the image (contrast, brightness, hue, and so forth). You can also used this program to blur the edges of some of the images.

4. The following is a summary of the methods Carol used to print or photocopy images. In all cases, you can make efficient use of the pages by ganging multiple images when printing or copying.

a. Fabric sheets with a paper backing: After waiting for a minute or two for the ink to dry, peel off the paper backing. Attach it to your page by stitching it on, or use fusible webbing to iron it on. This method is good if you plan to place your images on top of a patterned background, because the pattern will not show through.

b. Fabric sheets with a fusible backing: Trim or cut out the images, and then iron these onto your fabric page. This method also works well if you are placing images on top of a patterned background, because the pattern will not show through.

c. Sheets of iron-on photo transfer paper: This process will reverse your image when the image is ironed on, so choose the "mirror" option on the printer or computer to correct for this. Once you've printed the image onto the paper, cut around it and place it, print side down, on your fabric page before ironing it. You'll need to use a solid-colored fabric for this process, since a fabric pattern will show through.

6. Transfers can be made directly onto a page, or you can iron the transfer onto a separate piece of fabric and use fusible webbing to attach it.

7. Use swatches of fabric to embellish a page, as you would use paper in traditional scrapbooking. These can be sewn on or ironed on with fusible webbing.

8. To embellish the pages further, use fusible webbing to attach ribbon, or sew it on by hand. Attach dimensional embellishments with tacky glue. Sew on buttons and small picture frames. Carol also added embroidery and vintage lace to her pages.

9. To add words, use rubber stamps and a permanent-ink stamp pad or rub-on letters. You can also print text onto a fabric sheet, and cut it out before sewing it on or adhering it with fusible webbing. Or use found text from garments or ribbons.

10. When you've finished creating the design on your pages, use an 8-inch square quilt ruler to

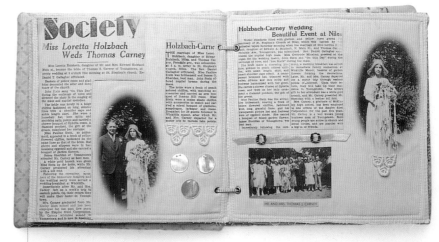

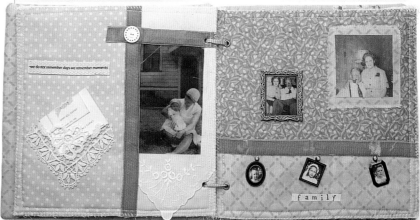

mark the boundaries of the finished pages with a fabric marking pencil. (Don't trim the fabric yet.)

11. Once the pages are marked, layer two pages (back to back) with quilt batting between them. Pin them together, making sure the markings are aligned on the two pages. Sew ¼ inch inside the marked square. Once sewn together, cut along the marked line to create an 8-inch square page. Use your sewing machine to finish the edges with a zigzag stitch.

12. Use eyelets and ribbon to bind the book. Make a template from cardboard to mark the holes so they're in the same place on every page. Create holes in the fabric pages with a Japanese screw punch, and use an eyelet setter to attach the eyelets to each page. Assemble the fabric pages and covers and thread ribbons through the holes to bind them.

ARTIST: SARAH FISHBURN

"I wanted to create a fun and uncomplicated journal honoring my dad's childhood. He was such a cute kid, a typical all-American boy who grew up in a small town in northern Illinois during the 1930s and 1940s. Although these were pivotal times for the country, he lived the everyday life of a young boy. Finding this tin in which to keep pages and memorabilia was serendipitous, and I love using the loose pages because working with them is so easy."

—S.F.

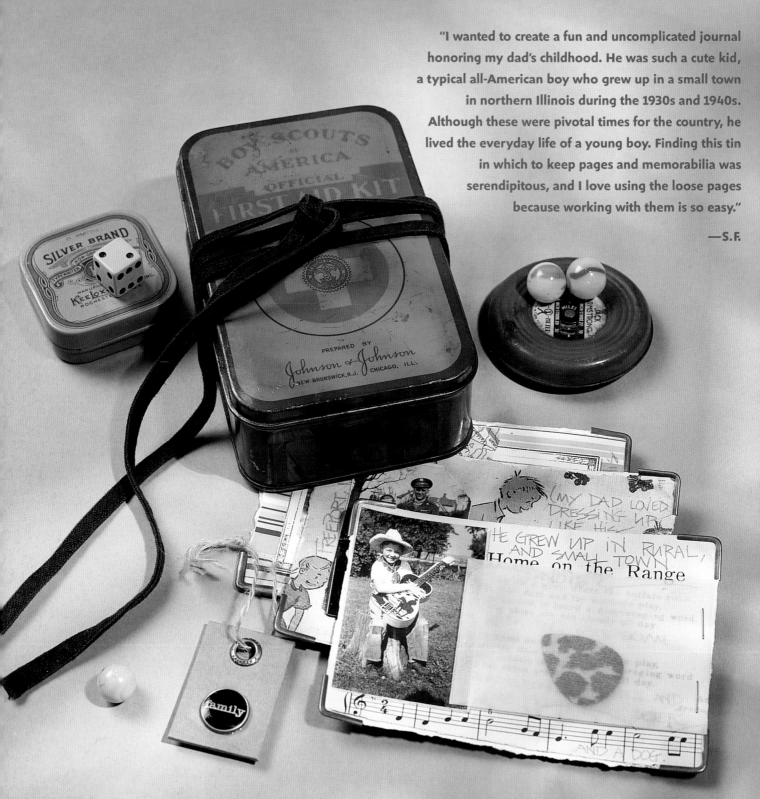

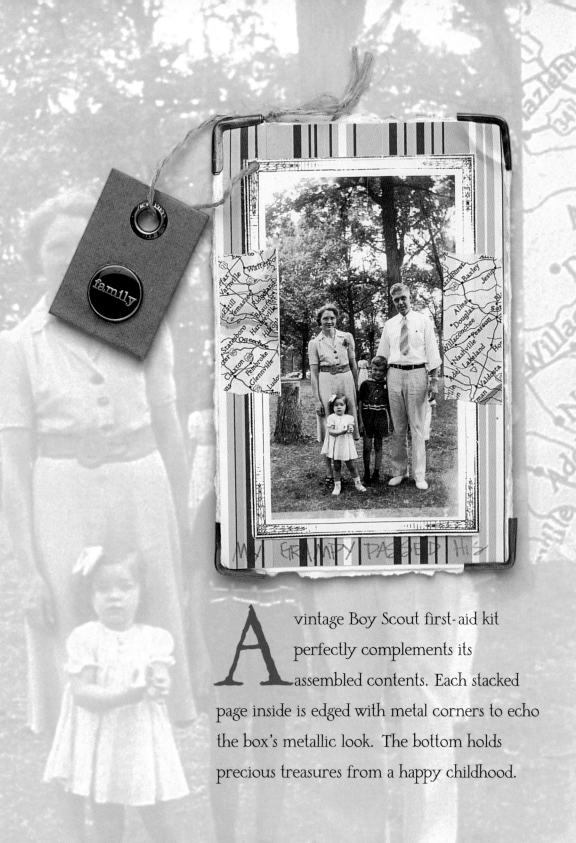

A vintage Boy Scout first-aid kit perfectly complements its assembled contents. Each stacked page inside is edged with metal corners to echo the box's metallic look. The bottom holds precious treasures from a happy childhood.

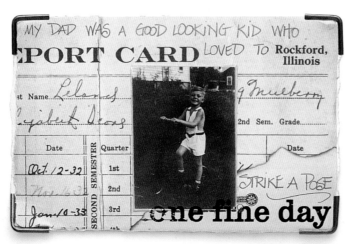

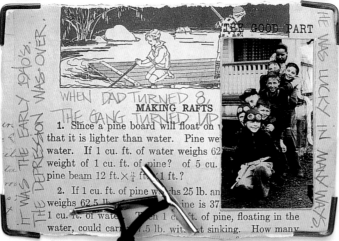

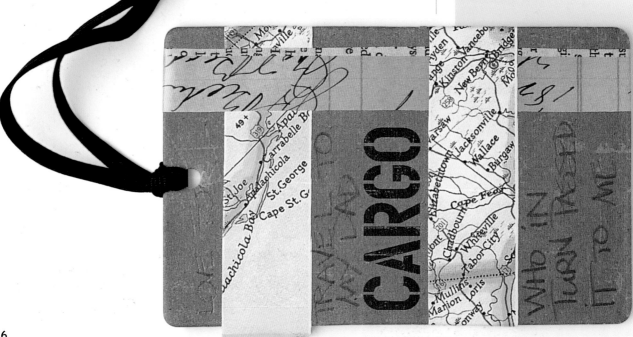

BOX

- Vintage box or tin
- Rub-on and sticker alphabet letters and words
- Cord

PAGES

- Watercolor paper
- Decorative notebook and found papers with vintage theme
- Mono-adhesive (available through art suppliers)
- Metal photo corners (available through scrapbooking suppliers)
- Photocopies of vintage images
- Yellow highlighting marker
- Embellishments such as index tabs, typewritten words, vellum envelopes, and vintage memorabilia

TOOLS

- Glue stick
- Metal straightedge
- Small hammer

PROCESS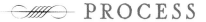

1. Decorate the outside of the box first. You can use rub-on letters to spell out your theme.

2. Tear the pieces of watercolor paper to fit inside the box. For consistency, it's helpful to tear the sheets underneath a metal straightedge.

3. Use the mono adhesive to attach bits of vintage paper with torn edges here and there to the front and back of the pages. Hammer metal corners to the page edges to protect them.

4. Fold the edges of the vintage images and tear them out instead of cutting them. Use a yellow highlighter to color some of the edges.

5. Adhere a photo to each page and add an embellishment or two. Finish the pages with a bit of penciled journaling. This informal scrapbook is a great place to incorporate some of your own, or your subject's, handwriting.

6. When you're finished decorating your pages, place them in the box and tie a cord around it, making it fun to open up.

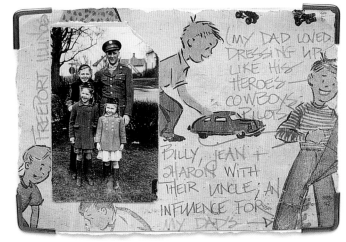

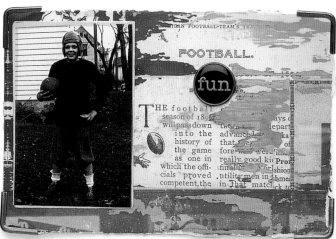

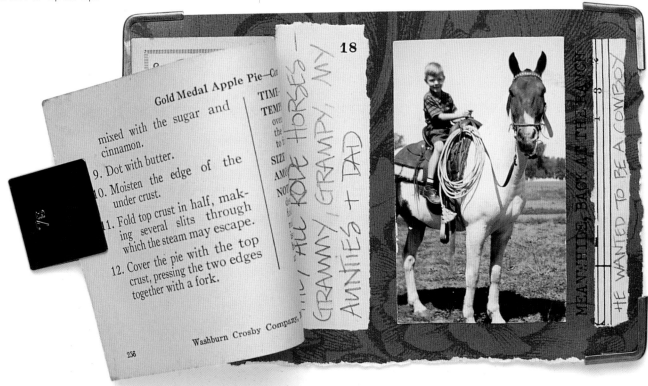

GRANDMOTHER'S VOYAGE TO ISRAEL

ARTIST: CLAUDIA LEE

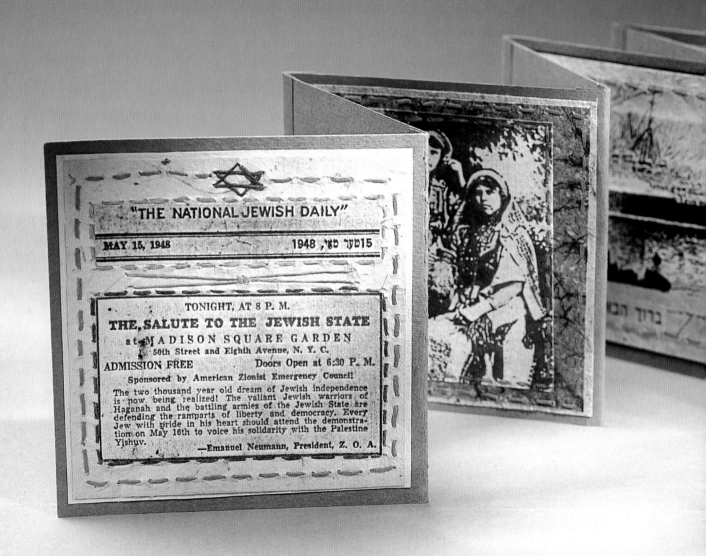

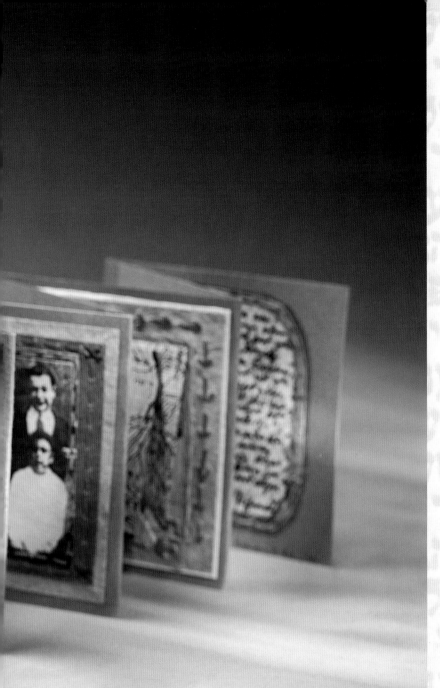

This moving chronology of images and text unfolds to show glimpses of a grandmother's voyage to her birthplace of Israel. The artist photocopied images and text onto her own handmade papers before coloring them with pencils. Stitching is used to highlight and delineate elements, as well as add color, texture, and visual interest.

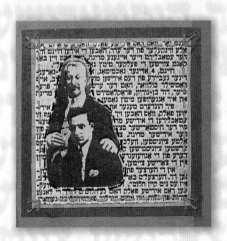

"This book commemorates my grandmother's trip to Israel in 1951, after it was proclaimed a state in 1948. I chose a concertina/accordion book form because it unfolds, two pages at a time, revealing the entire journey. The text is a mixture of the journal my grandmother Esther kept, a 1948 map of Jerusalem, and stories from the Jewish-American newspaper concerning the birth of the new state. Also included are photos of my grandparents and some of my cousins in Israel. On the back of each page is a line or two of text explaining that page." —C.L.

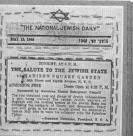
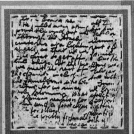
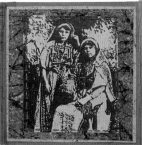
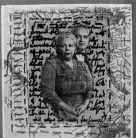
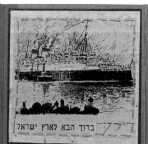
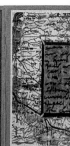

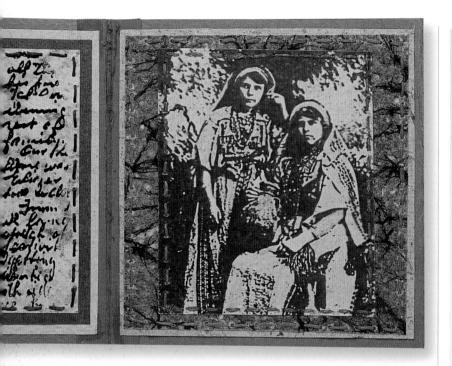

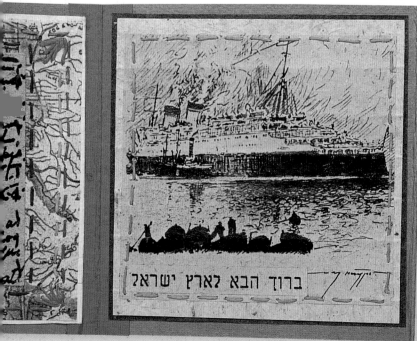

BOOK

- Heavy craft paper or cardstock
- Craft paper (for hinges)
- Double-sided tape

PAGES

- Handmade paper or other textured paper of your choice
- Various papers to use for backgrounds
- Matte fixative acrylic spray (available through art suppliers)
- Colored pencils
- Waxed linen in various colors

TOOLS

- Paper cutter or craft knife with fresh blades
- Bone folder
- Photocopier
- Small awl or needle tool and punching mat
- Size 18 sewing needle
- Computer and printer (for captions)

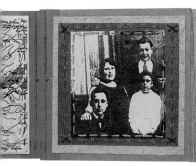

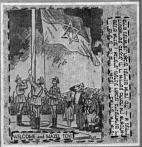
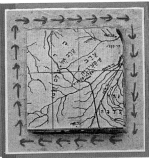
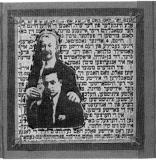
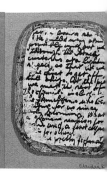

PROCESS

1. Claudia made this simple accordion-fold book from heavy craft paper bought from a factory closing sale, but you can use any heavy card stock or craft paper to make the book.

2. Cut the paper to the length and width of your book using a paper cutter or craft knife. If you need to join sections of cut paper because the paper you're using isn't long enough, you can make hinges out of craft paper or another strong paper. With the sections laid flat, attach the hinges to both sides of the sections/pages with double-sided tape. Use a bone folder to score and fold the pages.

3. To decorate the pages, photocopy text and images onto trimmed handmade paper. Make several samples until you like the way the images look.

4. After photocopying the images, spray a matte fixative over them to prevent smudging. To lend them a hand-tinted quality, add color to some of them with colored pencils.

5. Layer the text, images, background papers, and adhere all the papers with double-sided tape.

6. On top of a punching mat, use an awl to punch the stitching holes around the assembled papers, prior to mounting them on the book pages. With waxed linen, stitch from back to front, leaving the tail free on the back when you are done. Attach the finished piece to the page.

7. On the back of the piece, Claudia added computer-generated captions.

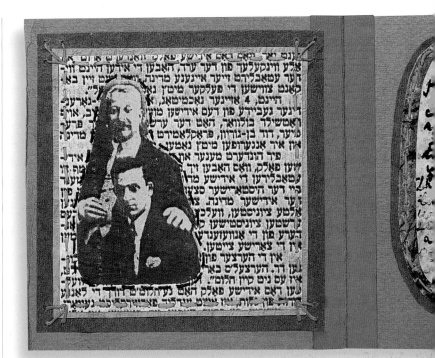

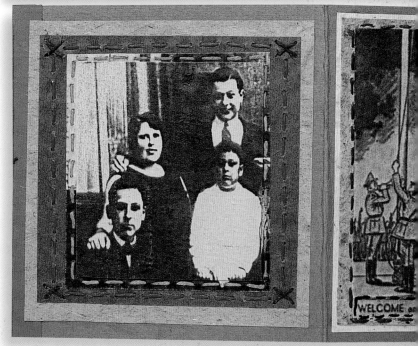

SNAPSHOTS OF MY LIFE

ARTIST: GWENDOLYN TAYLOR

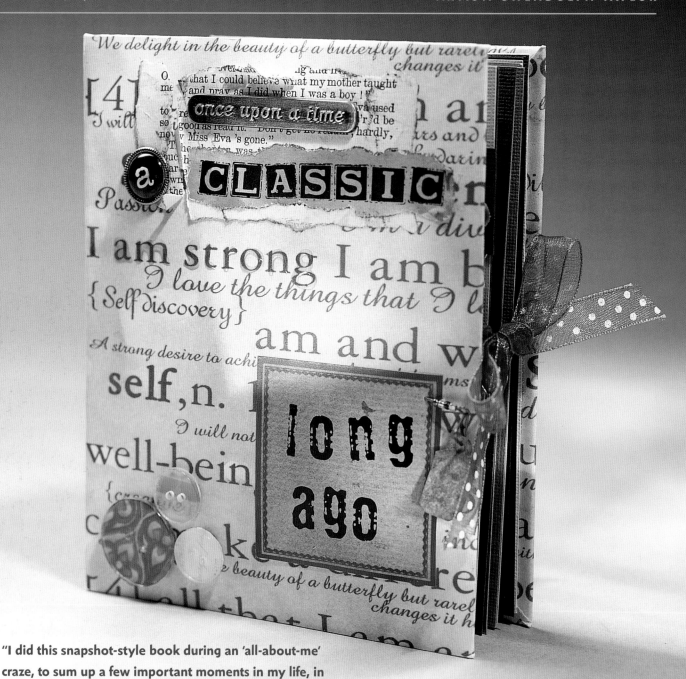

"I did this snapshot-style book during an 'all-about-me' craze, to sum up a few important moments in my life, in case I never created an in-depth book. It simply says, 'Hey, I was here, and I lived a little!'" —G.T.

The simple concertina-fold spine of this book lends it a special touch. Each signature folds out to show glimpses of the artist's life. Her casual approach makes the book accessible and fun.

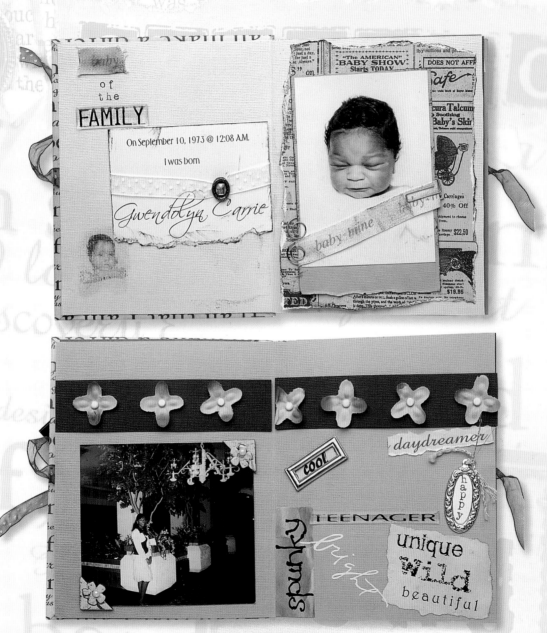

BOOK

- Patterned paper
- Chipboard
- Low-loft cotton batting
- White craft glue (PVA)
- Cardstock
- Ribbon

PAGES

- Embellishments such as metal charms, small frames, and fabric flowers
- Paper ephemera
- Stickers
- Photocopies of images

TOOLS

- Craft knife
- Bone folder
- Blender pen

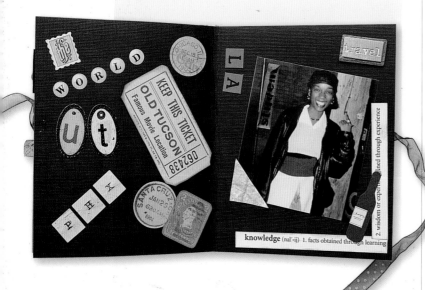

 PROCESS

1. Fold an 8½ x 5½-inch sheet of patterned paper in the middle to begin a simple concertina fold for the book's spine. Use the bone folder to create ½-inch fanlike folds.

2. To make the covers, cut two pieces of chipboard, each 5 x 6 inches. Trim two pieces of patterned paper to 6 x 7 inches each. Glue a layer of low-loft cotton quilt batting to one side of a piece of chipboard to serve as your front cover.

3. Place each piece of chipboard face down on a piece of patterned paper, score along all four edges and miter each corner, leaving enough margin to cover the edges. Fold the paper over the edges and glue it down. Cut a length of ribbon in half, and glue each end to the middle of the covers to serve as the book's closure.

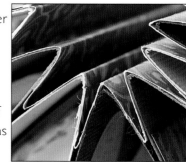

4. Adhere the edge of the accordion-folded sheet to the edge of one of the covers. Apply glue to the edge of the other cover and adhere the spine.

5. Fold pieces of cardstock in half to fit inside the folds of the spine. Apply adhesive to each valley of the fold, and glue the sheets inside. After all signatures are glued in place, adhere the first and last pages to the inside covers.

6. With this type of book, you can attach embellishments to the page with brads and eyelets or do stitching, and then glue the pages together back-to-back to hide the finishes.

7. Embellish the covers and pages with photo transfers made with a blender pen, ephemera ribbons, fabric flowers, small metal frames, and stick-on letters of various types.

SCHOOL DAZE

ARTIST: SARAH FISHBURN

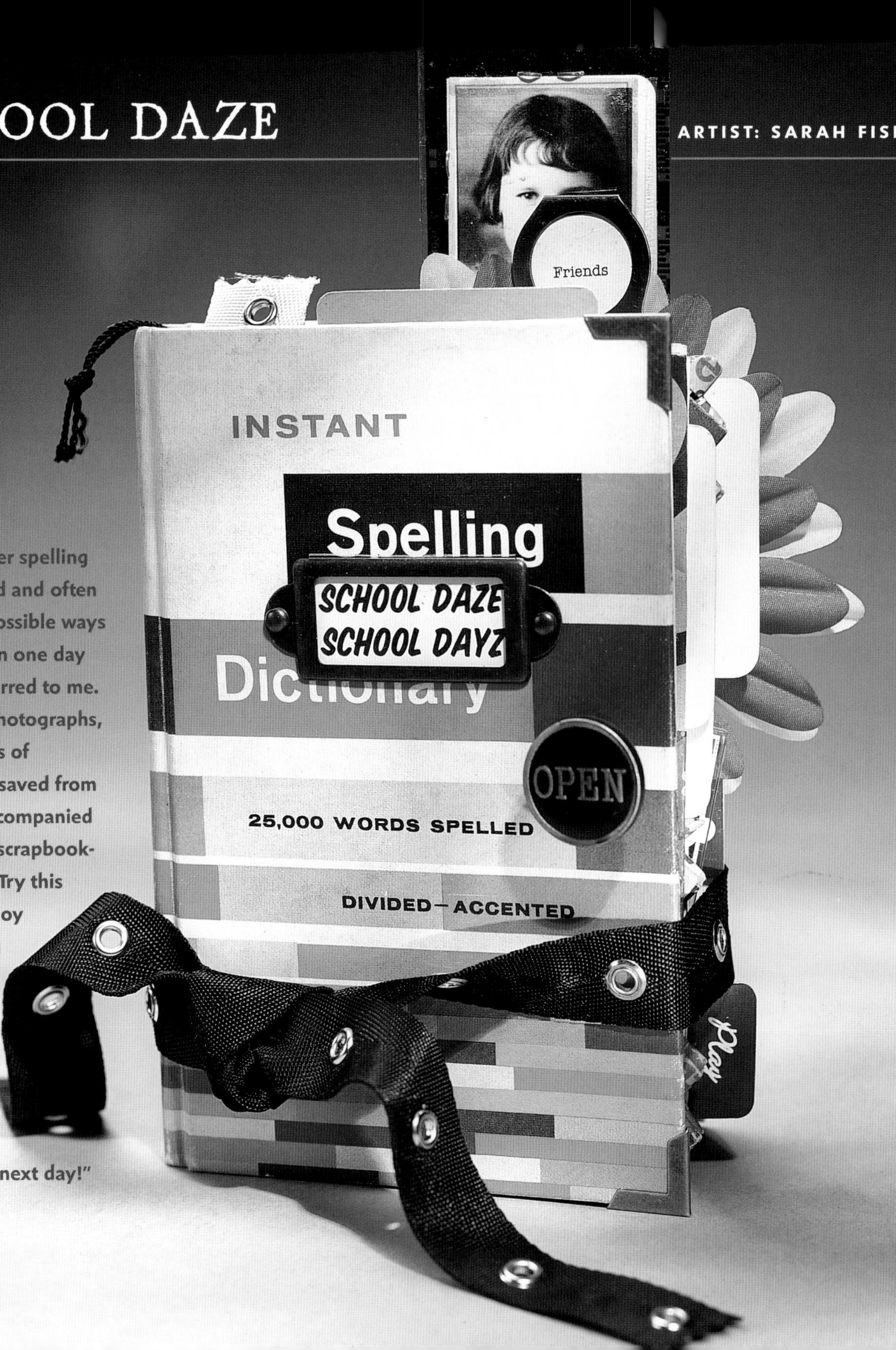

"I had an older spelling book on hand and often considered possible ways to use it. Then one day this idea occurred to me. Along with photographs, I included bits of memorabilia saved from years ago, accompanied by some fun scrapbooking supplies. Try this and you'll enjoy remembering a simpler time, when your biggest worry was (hopefully) what to pack for lunch the next day!"
—S.F.

Friends

INSTANT

Spelling

SCHOOL DAZE
SCHOOL DAYZ

Dictionary

OPEN

25,000 WORDS SPELLED

DIVIDED–ACCENTED

Play

What a clever way to enjoy school photos or snapshots! Find a fun textbook from approximately the same era as the photographs, and use it to make an altered journal. Each two-page spread carries a single "girlfriend" theme.

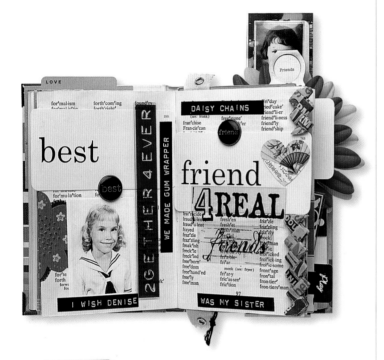

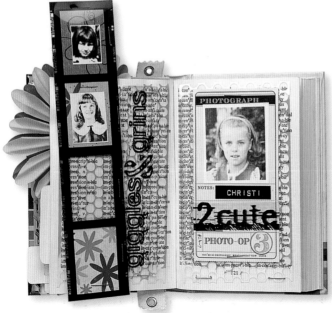

BOOK AND PAGES

- Old book
- Photocopies and computer-altered versions of photos
- Mono adhesive (adhesive strip available through art suppliers)
- Colored pencils
- A variety of decorative papers and wrapping papers, including printed cellophane
- Stickers and labeling tape
- Faux strips resembling photo negatives
- Sequin waste (remainder sheets from punched sequins)
- Rickrack, twill tape with grommets, and decorative tapes
- Embellishments such as decorative brads, plastic and fabric flowers, fabric scraps, found memorabilia, index tabs, typewritten words, epoxy words, label frames, and see-through acrylic frames

TOOLS

- Computer and photo-altering program
- Label-maker
- Scissors or craft knife

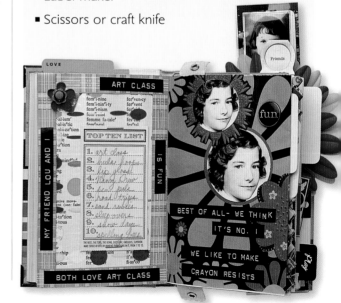

⟫⟫⟫⟫ PROCESS ⟪⟪⟪⟪

1. Cover some pages of your book with background papers or allow some of the words to peek through layers on parts of the page. Before laying out the pages, Sarah added hand coloring to a few of my photocopies and altered other images on a computer.

2. Work on each two-page spread at a time, laying the photos out with a combination of both scrapbooking elements and memorabilia. Use mono-adhesive to attach these elements to the pages. Add a few dimensional elements, and use the label-maker to add a few words about each friend.

3. Sarah added a small door pull to the cover that says "OPEN". She also placed the name of the book in a label frame and adhered it to the front.

4. Don't hesitate to experiment with lots of elements and layers...the more the merrier! Allow layers to stick out from the pages, creating an edge that invites touching.

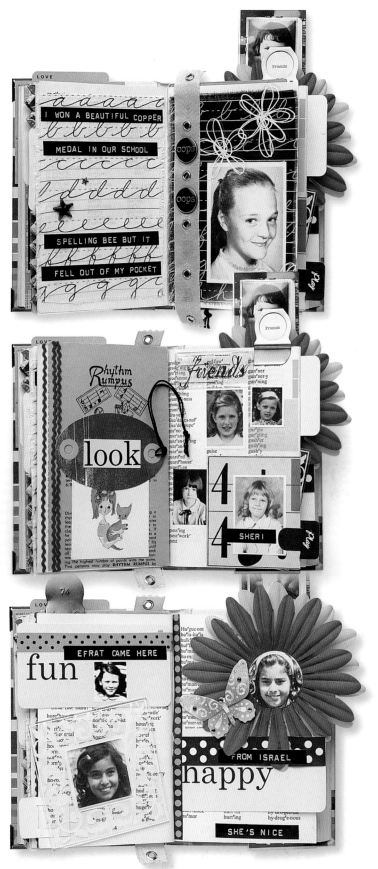

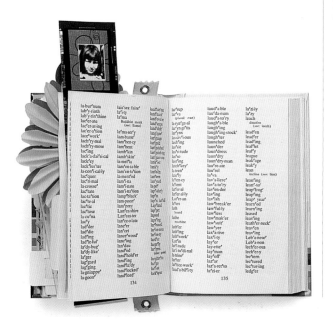

MY FAMILY'S MUSICAL JOURNEY

ARTIST: DANA IRWIN

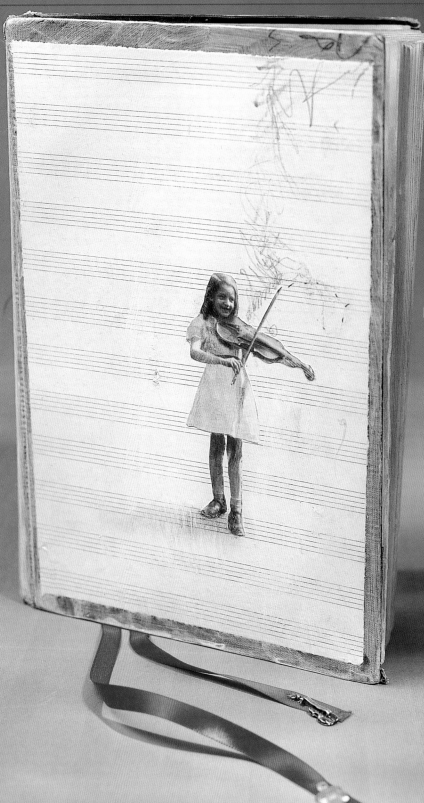

"This book is a tribute to my mother's musical influence on those around her—from Brownie troops she led, to the orchestra in which she played first violin for 30 years. Music was, and still is, a central part of our family gatherings. I selectively chose items for this book that capture memories from each decade of our lives together." —DI

Since the late 1880s, Dana's family has been recording events through photographs, and she had a lot of photographic imagery from which to choose. She wanted to assemble some of these bits and piece in a meaningful way. Her imaginative solution—she used an old music book as the substrate for holding this wonderful collection of images, ephemera, and memorabilia commemorating her musical heritage.

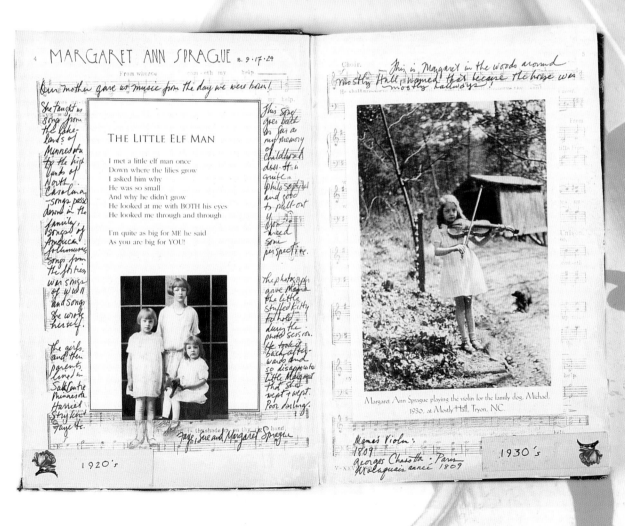

MARGARET ANN SPRAGUE B. 9·17·24

Our mother gave us music from the day we were born!

She taught us songs from the lakelands of Minnesota to the high lands of North Carolina, —songs passed down in the family, songs of American folkmusic, songs from the Shakers, war songs of WWII and songs she wrote herself.

The girls and their parents lived in SaukCentre Minnesota. Harriet Strykert Faye &c.

THE LITTLE ELF MAN

I met a little elf man once
Down where the lilies grow
I asked him why
He was so small
And why he didn't grow
He looked at me with BOTH his eyes
He looked me through and through

I'm quite as big for ME he said
As you are big for YOU!

This song goes back as far as my memory of childhood does. It is quite a philosophical and good to pull out when you need some perspective.

The photograph gave Margie the little stuffed kitty to hold during the photo session. He took it back afterwards and so disappointed little Margaret that she wept + wept. Poor darling.

Faye, Sue and Margaret Sprague

1920's

This is Margaret in the woods around Mostly Hall, named that because the house was mostly hallways!

Margaret Ann Sprague playing the violin for the family dog, Michael, 1930, at Mostly Hall, Tryon, NC.

Mama's Violin:
1809
Georges Chanotta · Paris
Mirecourt année 1809

1930's

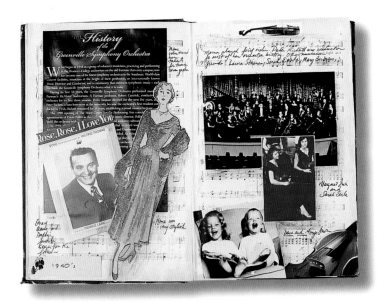

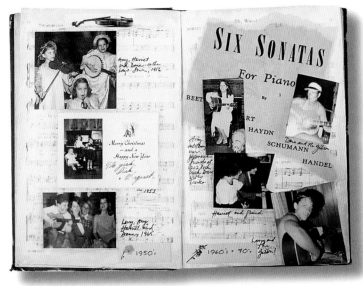

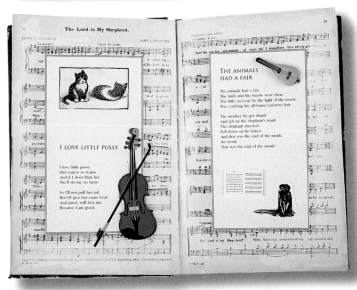

- Old music book
- Memorabilia such as musical scores and photos from old magazines
- Ephemera such as tiny replicas of instruments, strings from old instruments, and guitar picks
- Photocopies
- White craft glue
- Ink pen
- White acrylic paint
- Soft leaded pencil

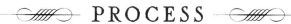

PROCESS

1. Find an old book that you want to use as your substrate from a used bookstores or second-hand store.

2. On the cover of her book, Dana glued musical staffs and a beautiful photo of her mother playing the violin. To accentuate this detail, she used a pen to draw sound marks resonating from her bow.

3. Prepare the inside pages by gluing several sheets together with watered-down glue. By doing this, you'll create thicker and sturdier pages for holding collage elements and memorabilia. Allow the pages to dry thoroughly.

4. Assemble your photocopies of images along with memorabilia and create interesting visual passages that describe events and feelings. Add handwritten text that describes your memories.

5. When the pages are laid out, whitewash them with thinned-down white acrylic paint, softening the overall look of the pages.

6. Add shading with a soft leaded pencil to lend the pages depth.

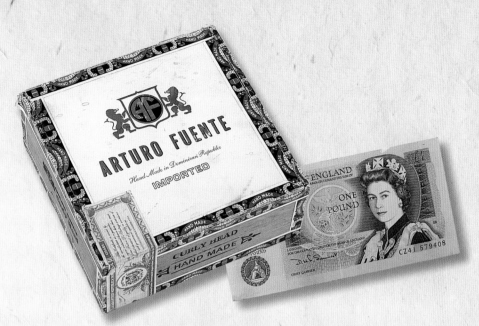

EXPLORE

While exploring a new place, allow yourself to see new possibilities for artistic expression. Traveling can open your mind to new cultures, as well as materials, so collect things along the way to assemble into a book that reflects an adventurous outlook.

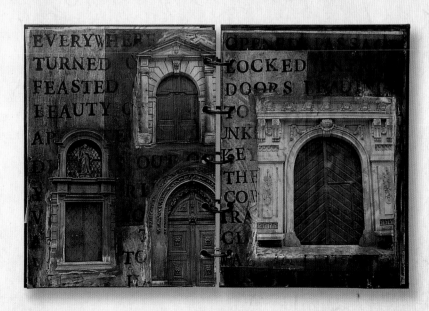

"DIOS DE LA MUERTE" MEMORY BOOK

ARTISTS: OPIE AND LINDA O'BRIEN

"We enjoy leading workshops in faraway places, and one of our favorite spots is Puerto Vallarta, Mexico. In this book, we decided to document some nights out on the town, including The Day of the Dead festivities. An unusual clipboard found at a garage sale inspired us, and we decorated the outside of it with tin cans, metal eyelet lettering, and glass embellishments. We added found objects and memorabilia to an arsenal of small photos, and used portable media such as rubber stamps and colored pencils to decorate the pages." —L.O.

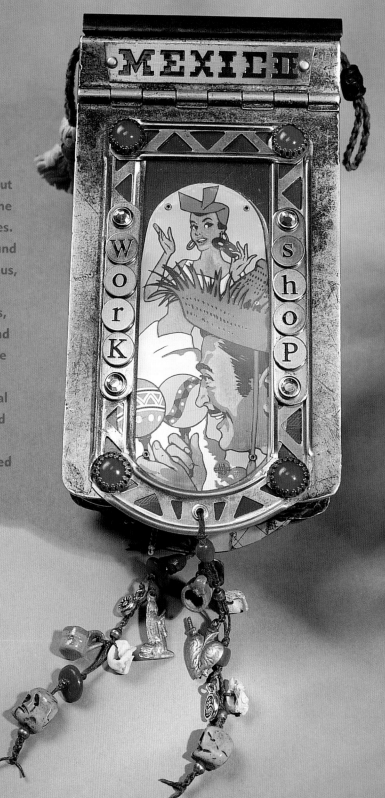

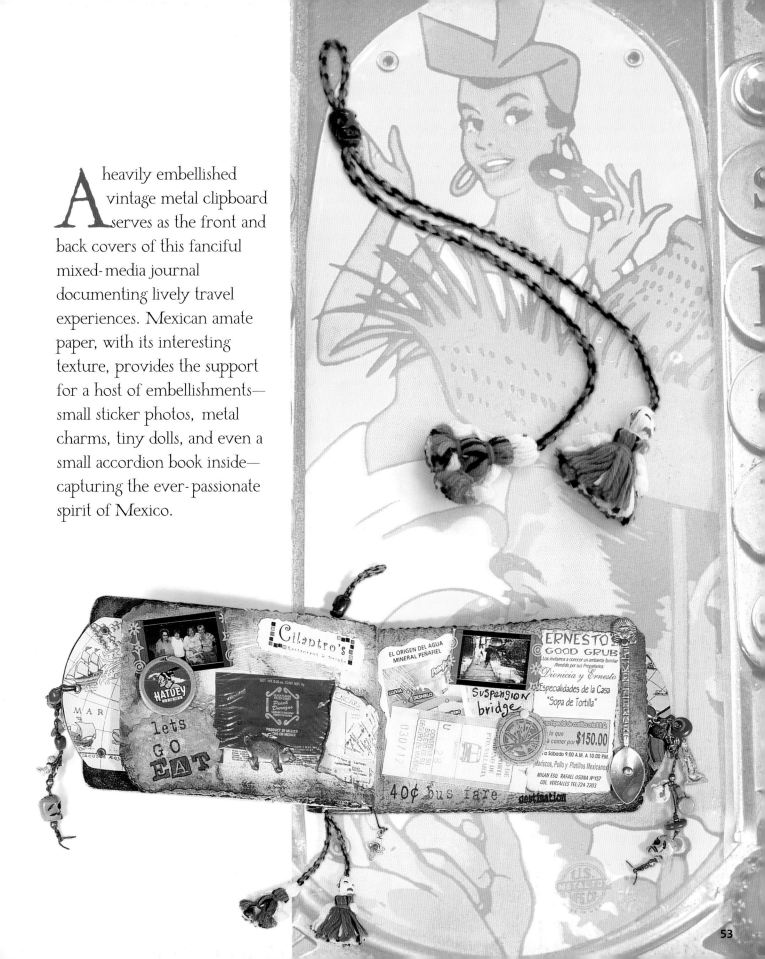

A heavily embellished vintage metal clipboard serves as the front and back covers of this fanciful mixed-media journal documenting lively travel experiences. Mexican amate paper, with its interesting texture, provides the support for a host of embellishments— small sticker photos, metal charms, tiny dolls, and even a small accordion book inside— capturing the ever-passionate spirit of Mexico.

COVERS

- Clipboard with built-in spring clamp mechanism
- Embellishments: images cut from tin cans, pieces from a vintage metal erector set, copper bezel cups, glass cabochons, metal eyelet letters, and beaded dangles on waxed linen thread
- Strong bonding glue
- $\frac{1}{8}$-inch eyelets

PAGES

- Mexican amate (bark) paper in various colors
- Double-faced tape, strong bonding glue (for metal), wood glue, eyelets and brads, washers, and waxed linen
- Images cut from tin cans
- Airbrush markers and distress inks
- Colored pencils and water-soluble crayons
- Reduced photos, including digital and small sticker photos taken with an instant camera
- Embellishments such as assorted rubber-stamped images, stickers, metal eyelet phrases and letters, metal eyelets and brads, Milagros, and other assorted found objects
- Shrink plastic ink-jet sheets

TOOLS

- Metal-edged snips
- Dremel or rotary tool with drill bits to fit eyelets and brads
- Deckle-edged rotary cutter and self-healing mat
- Japanese screw punch and thin awl
- Eyelet setter and hammer with steel block
- Computer, scanner, photo-editing program, and printer

 # PROCESS

1. To decorate the clipboard covers, Linda and Opie used bits and pieces of an old toy erector set to frame images snipped from colorful tin cans. To attach the metal pieces to a metal surface, use extra-long $\frac{1}{8}$-inch eyelets set in holes drilled with a rotary tool. Metal eyelet letters were glued to the edges, and the corners of the frame were accented with metal bezel cups holding red and blue glass cabochons. String beads and dangles onto waxed linen to accentuate the closure.

2. To make each page, they joined together two colored amate papers with sheets of double-faced adhesive. Then they used a deckle-edged rotary cutter to trim the page edges. The edges are high-lighted with airbrush markers and/or distress inks.

3. All of the page embellishments (photos, plastic tiles, tin, found objects, beads, etc.) can be attached with a combination of double-faced tape, brads, eyelets, washers, wood glue, and waxed linen. Colored pencils, water-soluble crayons, and rubber-stamped images are used on some pages to add words and/or designs.

4. To create shrink plastic image tiles, you can scan and size photos and various paper ephemera before printing them out on shrink plastic ink-jet sheets. Use a Japanese screw punch to make holes in them and attach them with brads.

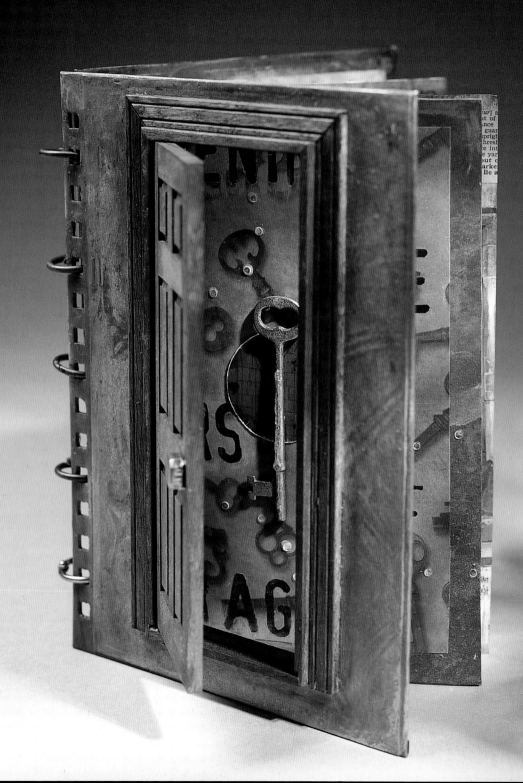

This book is made from a simple wire-bound notebook. Once the wire was removed and the loose pages decorated, metal O-rings were used to secure them. This construction allows pages to be added and removed with ease. The moveable dollhouse door on the cover ties in directly with the theme, inviting the viewer to enter and explore the book.

"During a vacation in Prague, my husband and I strolled the streets searching for things to photograph that might capture our unique experience there. A beautiful old door in our neighborhood caught our attention, and we stopped to take a picture. From intricately carved wood and ornately shaped iron designs to industrial models covered in layers of graffiti, each door held a unique sense of voice, reflecting the city's complex character. " —N.M.

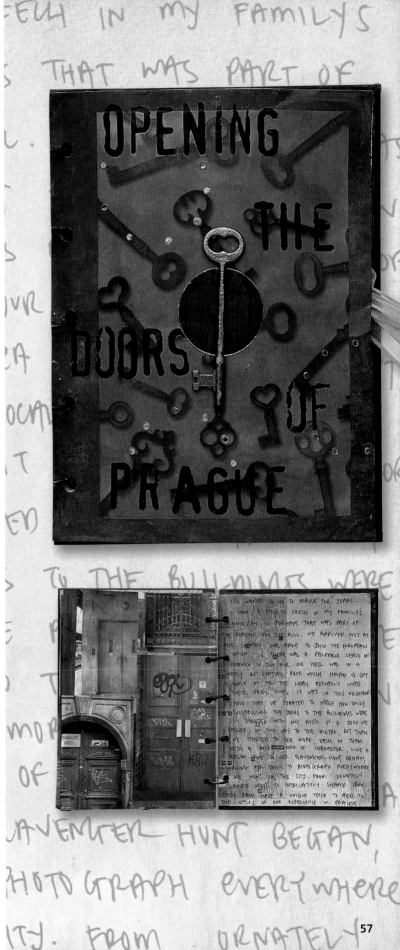

COVER

- Spiral-bound notebook
- Dollhouse door (available at craft supply stores)
- Acrylic paints
- Metal O-rings

PAGES

- Color photocopies or computer printouts of photos
- Photocopies of word definitions or other theme-related material
- Found object, such as a metal key, for opening page
- Strong bonding adhesive
- White craft glue (PVA)
- Alphabet stamps and stamp pad
- Oil pastels
- Scrapbook papers and cardstock
- Decorative ribbons or bits of fabric
- Beeswax

TOOLS

- Needle-nose pliers or small pair of household pliers
- Hole punch
- Craft knife
- Dedicated metal tin, brush, heat gun, and ventilator mask (for beeswax)

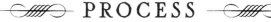 PROCESS

1. Use pliers to remove the wire spiral from your notebook by grabbing the free end of it before twisting it out. Remove several of the inside pages and set the others aside. The pages will bulk up substantially as you embellish them, so you'll only need a few to fill the space between the covers.

2. Because of her theme, Nicole chose to add a hinged dollhouse door to the cover. She cut a hole in the cover before using strong bonding adhesive to attach it along the cut edges. She painted around it with acrylic paint to give it a rustic appearance, and painted the back cover with the same tones.

3. After they're completely dry, set the covers aside and begin embellishing the pages. To fit her theme, Nicole glued an old key inside the door on the first page of her book.

4. Apply a decorative paper or photocopied text to the empty page as a background for your photos, or apply the photos directly to the page and add paint or other colored media around them. On some pages, Nicole used alphabet stamps to add words that evoked feelings about places she saw. She added oil pastel around the edges of the photos to create a nice effect. All of these approaches contribute to the idea of a pieced-together memory, rather than a formal, planned composition.

5. To create a small book within your book, fold together a booklet that fits inside the format of your page. Adhere images inside.

6. For a subtle effect, add a coat of beeswax to each page as you work. To do this, melt the wax in a dedicated metal tin before brushing layers of it onto the surfaces as you cover them. A heat gun comes in handy for removing brushstrokes. If you are using melted beeswax and/or a heat gun, always use a ventilator mask and work on a protected surface.

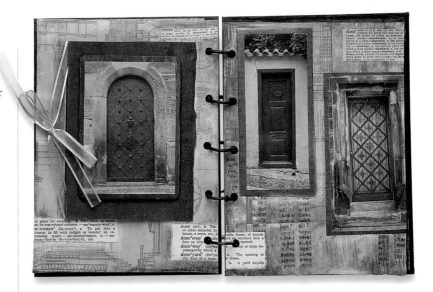

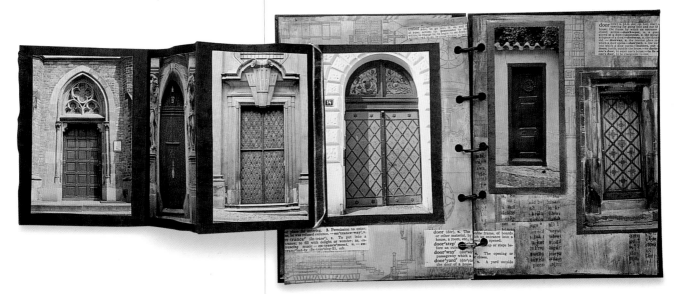

7. After all of your pages are covered, use the hole punch to punch holes that line up with those on the covers. (You can punch intermittent holes, leaving some of the original ones empty.) Assemble the pages between the two covers, and feed each onto the metal O-rings.

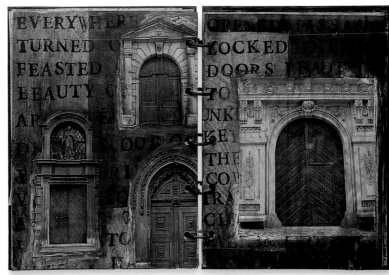

RWANDA 2005

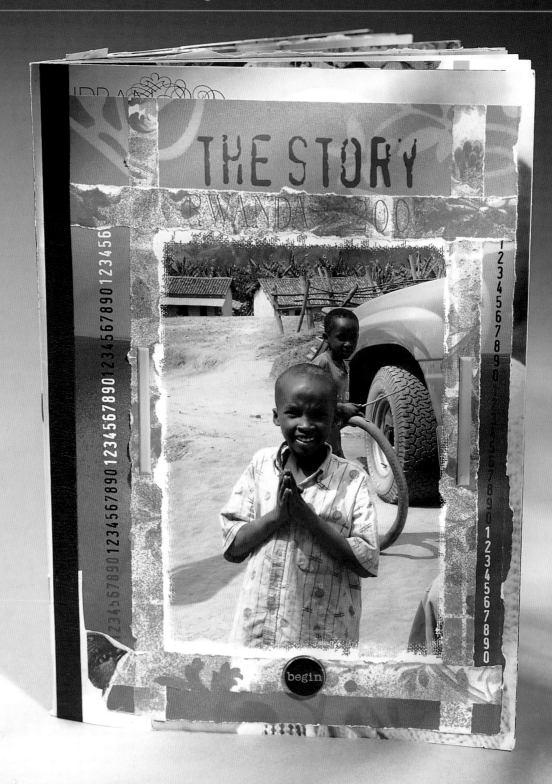

This eloquent presentation about a son's trip to "a land far, far away" is composed with both compassion and respect for the difficulties of a terribly impoverished environment. The artist approaches this subject with sensitivity and refinement, while capturing both joyous and poignant moments.

BOOK AND PAGES

- Mail-order or other disposable catalog

- Spray paint

- Stencils and masks: traditional alphabet, floral, geometric shapes, lace used as a stencil

- Watercolor paper, cardstock, decorative scrapbook papers, wrapping papers, scanned handmade paper, and torn pages from other catalogs

- Carpet-seaming tape and masking tape

- Photos

- Photocopy of map

- Mono-adhesive or glue stick

- Embellishments such as bar brads, decorative paper clips, fabric scraps, found memorabilia, glass tags, index tabs, typewritten words, and dimensional epoxy stickers

- Computer-generated journaling

- Labeling tape

- Rub-on alphabet letters, words, and numbers

TOOLS

- Scissors or craft knife

- Computer

- Label maker

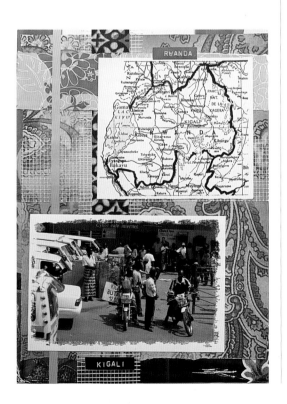

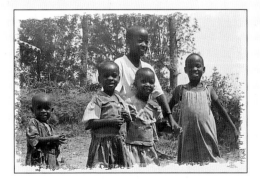

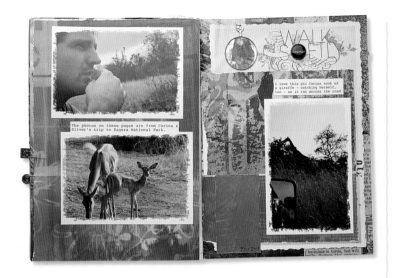

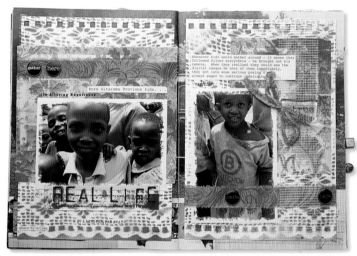

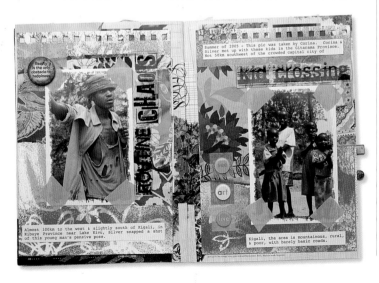

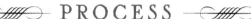

"My son Silver lived and worked in Rwanda, and my daughter Corina went to visit him for a time. When I saw their photos and heard their stories, it was like nothing I'd ever known. I was almost speechless at the extremes of beauty and ugliness, at the tragedy throughout the country, and yet...the triumph of humanity." —S.F.

PROCESS

1. Sarah began this project by using spray paint to stencil-paint some of the watercolor paper, cardstock, and decorative scrapbook papers.

2. To create a background for photos, collage pieces of painted and other papers directly onto the catalog covers and inside pages, leaving bits of the pages showing through here and there. Sarah added carpet-seaming tape as part of the background collages.

3. Pick one or two photos to focus on for each page, and attach them with mono-adhesive or a glue stick on top of the collaged papers. You can use torn strips of paper as borders for some of the photos or add bits of torn tape at each corner to create the look of an informal, bulletin board.

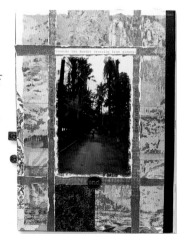

4. Embellish each page with a variety of textural elements. Tell a bit of your story on each page using a combination of labeling, epoxy stickers, rub-on letters, and computer-generated journaling.

WHEN IN ROME!

ARTIST: SUSAN MCBRIDE

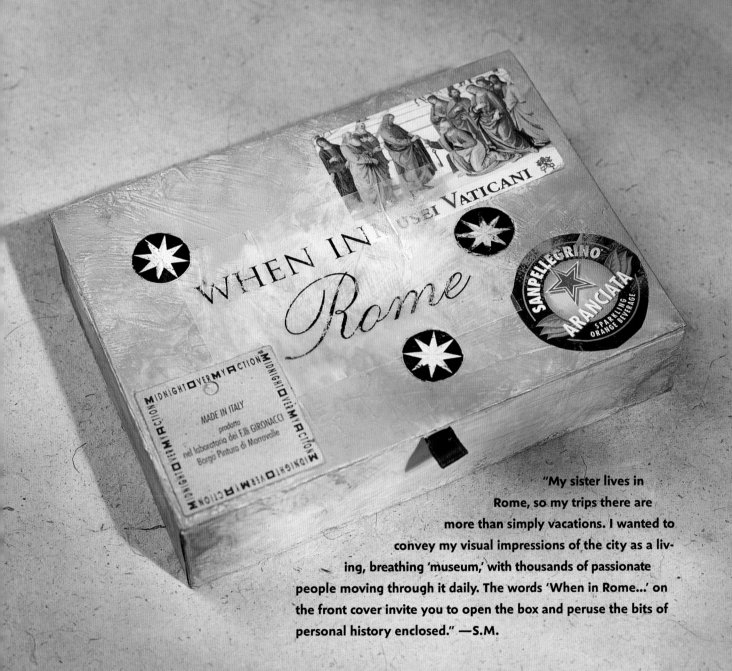

"My sister lives in Rome, so my trips there are more than simply vacations. I wanted to convey my visual impressions of the city as a living, breathing 'museum,' with thousands of passionate people moving through it daily. The words 'When in Rome...' on the front cover invite you to open the box and peruse the bits of personal history enclosed." —S.M.

Susan filled an empty card box with collaged images, memorabilia, and notes from her trip to Rome. This informal approach to scrapbooking can be done anywhere—you can even record your experiences as soon as you get your film developed. Expand the theme by decorating the container inside and out. Place a few precious found objects, such as coins or beach glass, in the bottom of the box.

BOX AND PAGES

- Sturdy box, such as a card or cigar box
- Card stock
- Photographs, clippings, food labels, and travel ephemera
- Double-sided tape or craft glue
- Acrylic paints
- Laser-friendly translucent vellum
- Gesso
- Acrylic matte medium

TOOLS

- Sharp scissors or craft knife
- Black pen
- Paintbrushes
- Computer and printer

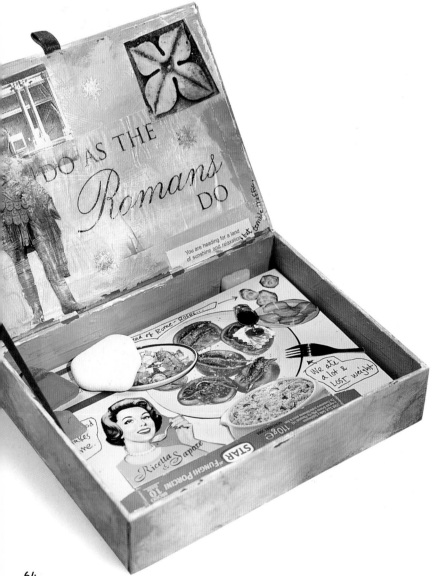

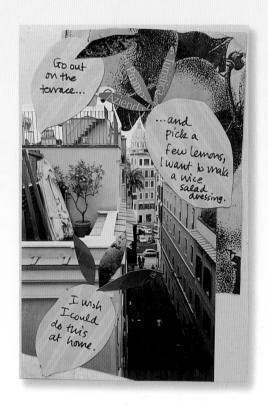

PROCESS

1. Trim pieces of cardstock to fit in the box's interior and serve as pages. Leave a margin around them so you can easily pull them out of the box.

2. Gather your photos, clippings, and ephemera. Cut out select portions of photos to silhouette, and attach them with small pieces of double-sided tape.

3. Use the pen to add commentary and a storyline around the images. Susan decided she wanted to take an informal "slice of life" approach to the city, so she recorded some anecdotes, based on some of her experiences. Continue adding cards to your collection as you record your impressions and exploits.

4. When Susan returned home, she prepared the box for decoration by covering the inside and outside with two coats of gesso to make a blank surface. Inspired by the antique walls of Rome, she layered several coats of acrylic paint on top of the gesso, wiping some of it off to reveal colors underneath. She printed text on some of the vellum sheets, then used acrylic matte medium to layer ephemera, clippings, and the printed vellum on the outside and inside of the box.

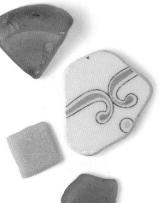

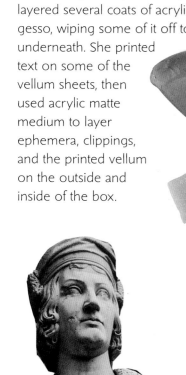

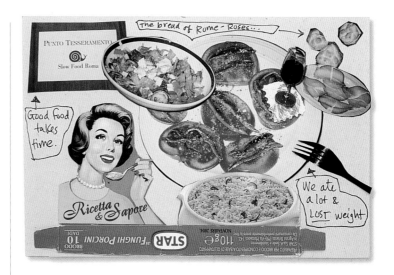

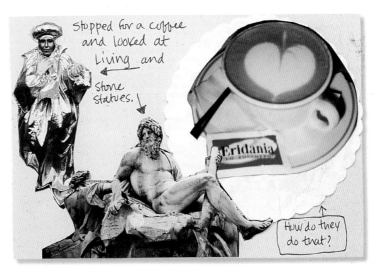

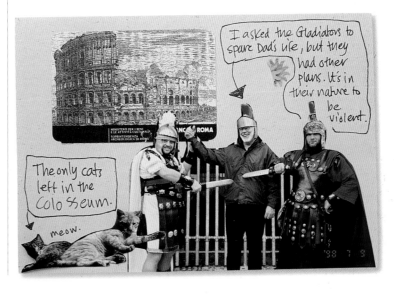

NOSTALGIC GRAND MESA VACATION

ARTIST: ERIKIA GHUMM

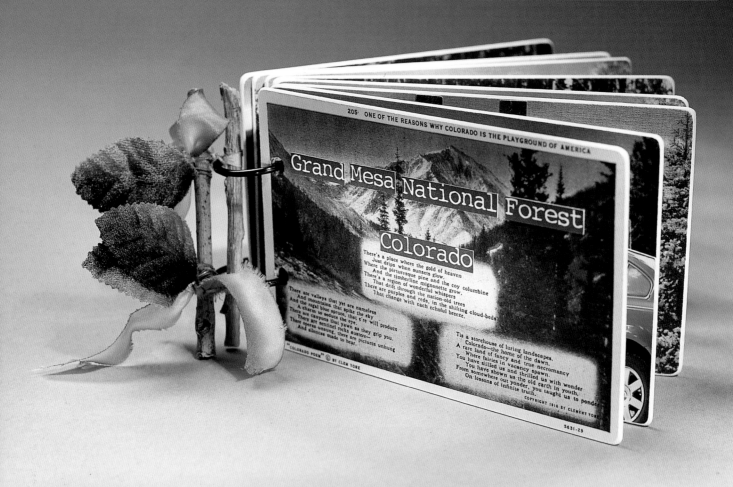

"On a trip, my husband and I drove through Grand Mesa National Forest and took a lot of photos. I thought, 'Why not combine the photos and vintage postcards into a kitschy scrapbook of our trip?' Because the postcards are beautiful on their own, I kept the album design fairly simple. I bound the pages with loose-leaf paper rings surrounded by two twigs adorned with velvety leaves and silk ribbon." —E.G.

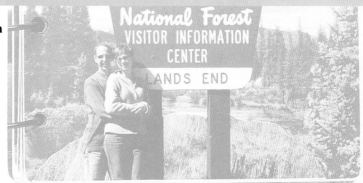

T he idea of combining images from vintage postcards with her own vacation photos occurred to the artist after she received a vintage card collection. After looking through lots of postcards, she found several showing her home state of Colorado 60 or 70 years ago. Overlaying nostalgic glimpses of the past with her vacation photos allowed her to combine two favorite concepts.

BOOK AND PAGES

- Vintage postcards
- White cardstock
- Mat board
- Sandpaper
- Ink-jet photo paper
- Solid sheet adhesive or other adhesive of your choice
- Loose-leaf paper rings, twigs, velvet leaves, and silk ribbon

TOOLS

- Computer, scanner, photo-editing program, and computer
- Sticker machine (optional)
- Scissors, craft knife, ruler, and cutting mat
- Hammer and anywhere (size adjustable) hole punch

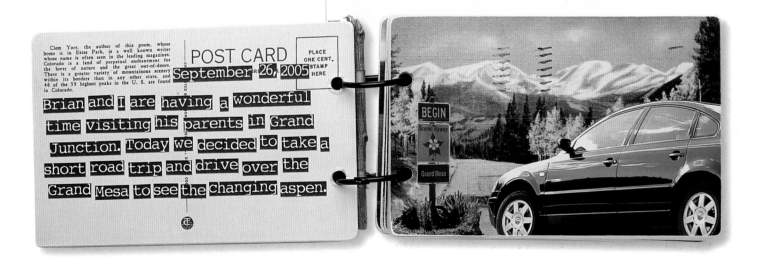

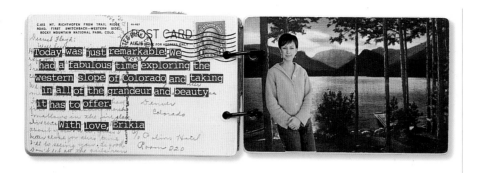

POST CARD

Today was just remarkable! We had a fabulous time exploring the western slope of Colorado and taking in all of the grandeur and beauty it has to offer.

With love, Erikia

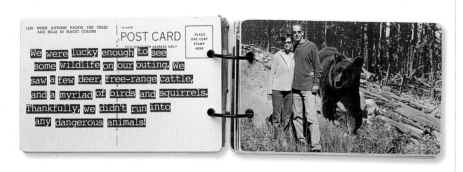

POST CARD

We were lucky enough to see some wildlife on our outing. We saw a few deer, free-range cattle, and a myriad of birds and squirrels. Thankfully, we didn't run into any dangerous animals!

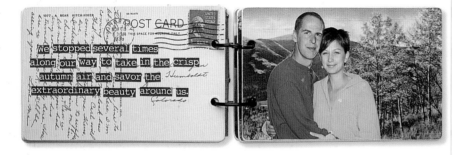

POST CARD

We stopped several times along our way to take in the crisp autumn air and savor the extraordinary beauty around us.

1. Scan the fronts and backs of your favorite postcards, and print them out on white cardstock. Apply adhesive to the backsides. Use the craft knife to cut them out.

2. Trim multiple pieces of mat board to postcard size, and adhere the postcard replicas to the fronts and backs. Use scissors to lightly trim the corners of the mat board, and sand the edges to smooth them out and lend the postcards a worn look.

3. Use a photo-editing program on your computer to crop your photos to fit onto the postcards. Print the images out on photo paper, and apply adhesive to the backs of them. Cut them out, silhouetting the images. Layer the photos on the postcards, and gently sand any resulting rough edges.

4. Mark the placement of your binding holes, and punch them out with the hole punch and hammer. On your computer, type journaling captions for the backs of the postcards, and print them out onto white cardstock. Back them with adhesive. Cut them out and layer them on the backs of the cards.

5. Bind the album with loose-leaf paper rings and twigs tied together with silk ribbon and velvet leaves.

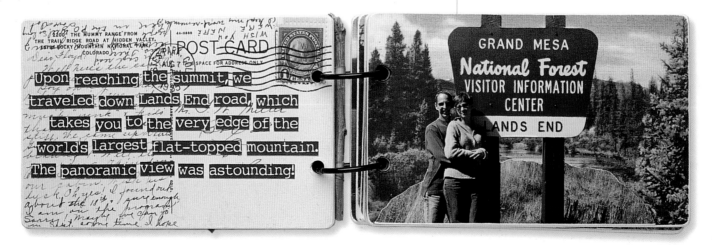

POST CARD

Upon reaching the summit, we traveled down Lands End road, which takes you to the very edge of the world's largest flat-topped mountain. The panoramic view was astounding!

GRAND MESA
National Forest
VISITOR INFORMATION CENTER
LANDS END

ADVENTUROUS CAMP DAYS

ARTIST: LISA W. COOK

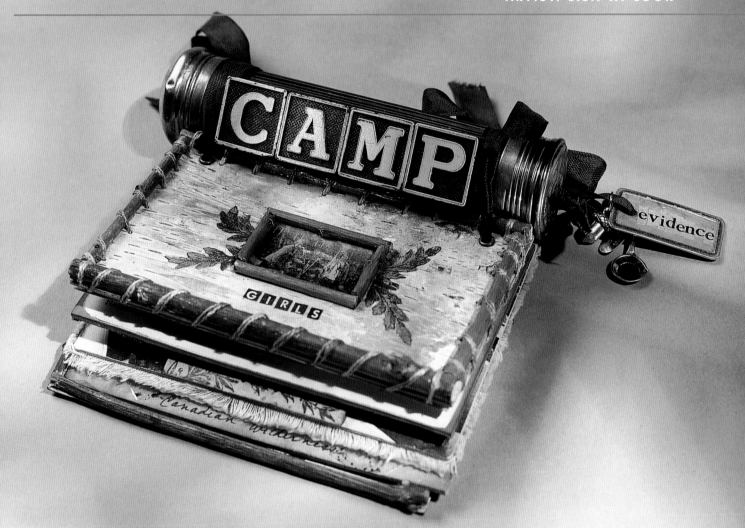

This unusual book began with the idea of using a vintage flashlight as a time capsule to hold a scrap of flannel and swatches from other clothing. From here, the artist was inspired to attach a scrapbook holding precious photos and memorabilia. The beautiful pages allow the viewer to experience the artist's very personal feelings surrounding a time of both innocence and growth.

after 10 days on the trail we craved certain foods and so a trip to Dairy Queen on the drive home was "heaven!"

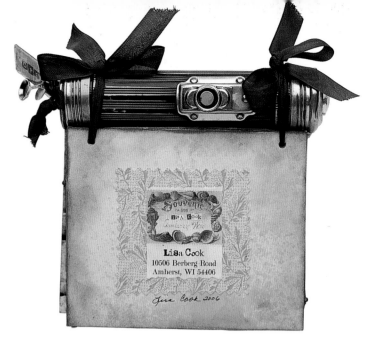

"The first time I went to summer camp, I hated it! I didn't pass the swimming test and had to stay in the shallow part of the lake. When I got older, camp was heaven. We took adventurous canoe trips, each a bit more challenging than the year before, until we were ready to canoe the Canadian Boundary Waters. I have very fond memories of bonding with a small group of girls as we challenged ourselves in the wilderness. Fortunately, my mother saved treasures from my adventures, so I was able to create a book filled with images, thoughts, and textures." —L.C.

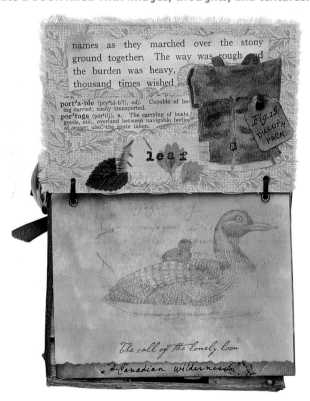

BOOK

- Mat board
- Vintage flashlight
- Rayon ribbon
- Anagram letter tiles

PAGES

- Reduced photocopies of photos
- Clear household caulk or heavy-duty adhesive
- Brown stamp pad
- Found birch bark
- Sticks or grapevine pieces
- Satin polyurethane varnish
- Linen thread
- Assorted fabrics
- Vintage ephemera
- Alphabet letters, stickers, tan tissue paper, and glassine envelope
- Mica sheet, charms, metal-rimmed tags, and aged shipping tags
- Thin tag board
- Eyelets

TOOLS

- Glue stick
- Craft knife and cutting mat
- Plastic spring clamps
- Hole punch
- Japanese screw punch with 2.5mm tip
- Sewing needle
- Eyelet setter and hammer
- Blender pen

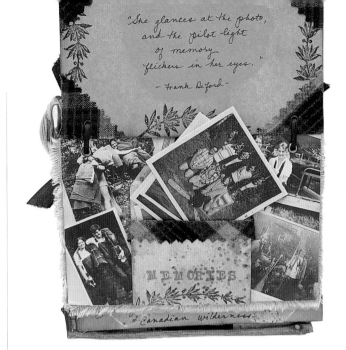

"She glances at the photo, and the pilot light of memory flickers in her eyes."

— Frank Deford —

PROCESS

1. Cut the covers and pages from the mat board. The book is made of two covers and two inside pages. Cut the cover (top piece) first and each subsequent piece slightly wider than the previous one to make an uneven edge.

2. Use a glue stick to attach the small paper items to the pages and caulk or heavy-duty adhesive to attach three-dimensional embellishments. Lisa decorated both the fronts and backs of the pages, and when the book is opened out, the pages relate nicely to one another. To "age" exposed page edges, she rubbed them with a brown stamp pad.

3. Lisa decorated the cover with a layer of birch bark adhered with clear caulk, and punched holes around the rim to hold linen thread. Then she cut the sticks to fit the four sides, glued them in place, and clamped them to dry. She sewed the border of thread through the holes on the cover, and varnished the threads and sticks before creating a small frame out of grapevine pieces to enclose a small sheet of mica covering a photo. A piece of thin tag board adhered to the back cover covers the stitching.

4. Use collage and scrapbooking elements to make up the pages particular to your theme. Some are suggested on the list above, but use whatever works for you. In one case, Lisa mounted tiny photos on tags and tucked them inside a glassine envelope before adhering it to a page.

5. After completing your decorated pages, place each on a cutting mat and punch two binding holes at the top with the Japanese screw punch. Set small eyelets in each hole.

6. Thread ribbon through the eyelets, and tie the pages to the body of the flashlight. Lisa adhered vintage-style letter tiles to the flashlight to spell "CAMP." She also dismantled the front lens of the flashlight and inserted a small photo behind the glass. A tag decorated with words is tied to the other end of the flashlight, inviting one to open the end and pull out the rolled-up treasures inside.

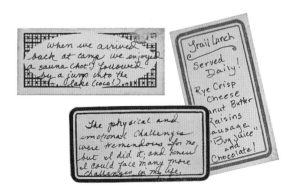

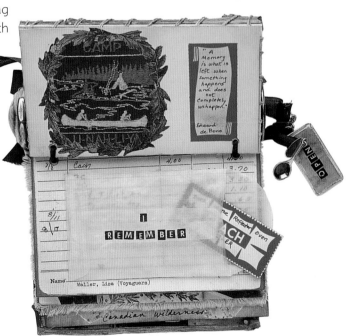

THE ADVENTURES OF CLAUDINE AND GEORGIE

ARTIST: CLAUDINE HELLMUTH

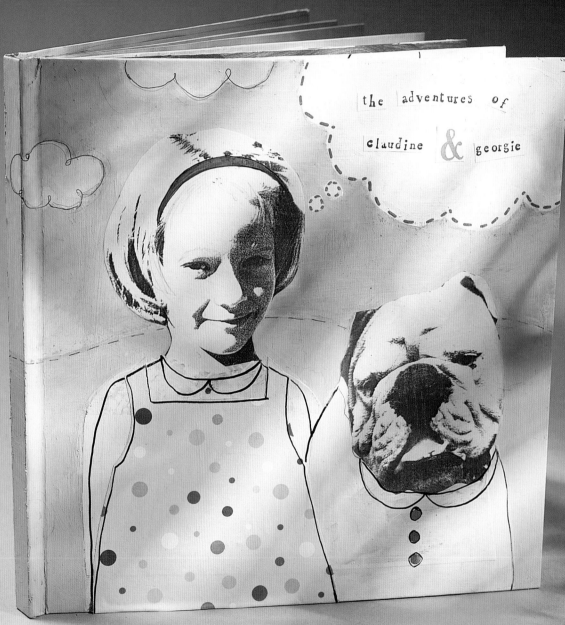

the adventures of claudine & georgie

"When I was a little girl, I had a bulldog named Georgie that I loved, so I decided to create a story about our adventures. I used old photos of the two of us, and cut out the heads to become part of an altered scrapbook. A children's pop-up book is the perfect structure, because it allows interactivity. It took a bit of thinking to decipher the existing pop-up structure and adjust my new elements to work with it." —C.H.

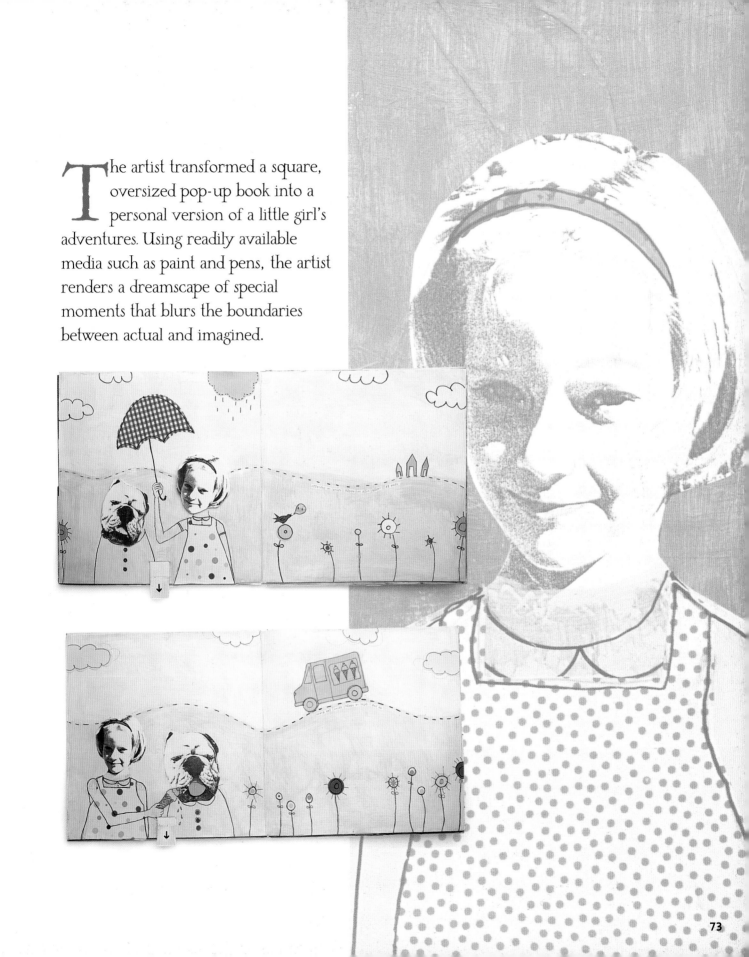

The artist transformed a square, oversized pop-up book into a personal version of a little girl's adventures. Using readily available media such as paint and pens, the artist renders a dreamscape of special moments that blurs the boundaries between actual and imagined.

BOOK

- Recycled pop-up book
- Sandpaper
- Gesso
- Acrylic paint
- Fabric and colored papers
- Black-and-white photocopies of photos
- Fine-tip black artist's pen
- Acrylic gel medium
- Heavy watercolor paper

TOOLS

- Craft knife or scissors
- Paintbrushes
- Typewriter or computer and printer

⚬⚬⚬ PROCESS ⚬⚬⚬

1. Claudine began by looking at each spread and the existing pop-up components. How could she alter and use the moving parts already in place? Once she figured this out, she was able to plan the compositional elements. She considered how my storyline could be carried out on the pages.

2. Before you begin altering the pages, sand each printed page lightly before applying a coat of gesso. Use a pencil to define the lines of your composition in the wet gesso.

3. Paint in basic backgrounds with acrylic paints. Cut out dress forms, birds, clouds, houses, flowers, and other shapes from fabric or paper. Use the acrylic gel medium to adhere these pieces on top of the painted background, and use a black pen to outline portions of the design.

4. Use acrylic gel medium to mount your photocopies on heavy watercolor paper, lending them extra stability. Cut out the images.

5. Trim away the main portion of the existing pop-up forms, leaving stems for attaching the new images. Glue the photo images to the stems so you're able to move them when you pull the tabs.

6. Use printed text to tell your story. Adhere it in appropriate places on your pages.

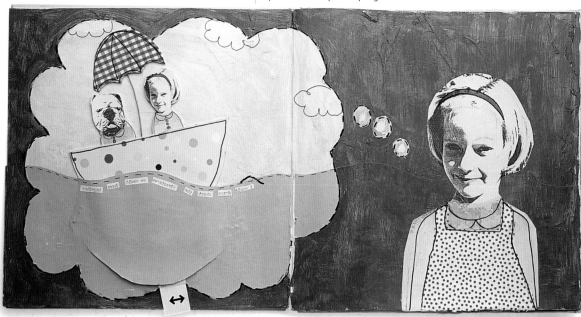

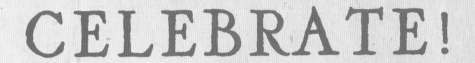

CELEBRATE!

From birthdays to reunions, no event in your life is too small to commemorate. Inspiration for your project can come from any type of celebration with family and friends. All you need to do is choose materials and techniques that help convey the emotion or theme of that celebration.

GIRL'S FANTASY

ARTIST: LINDA WARYLN

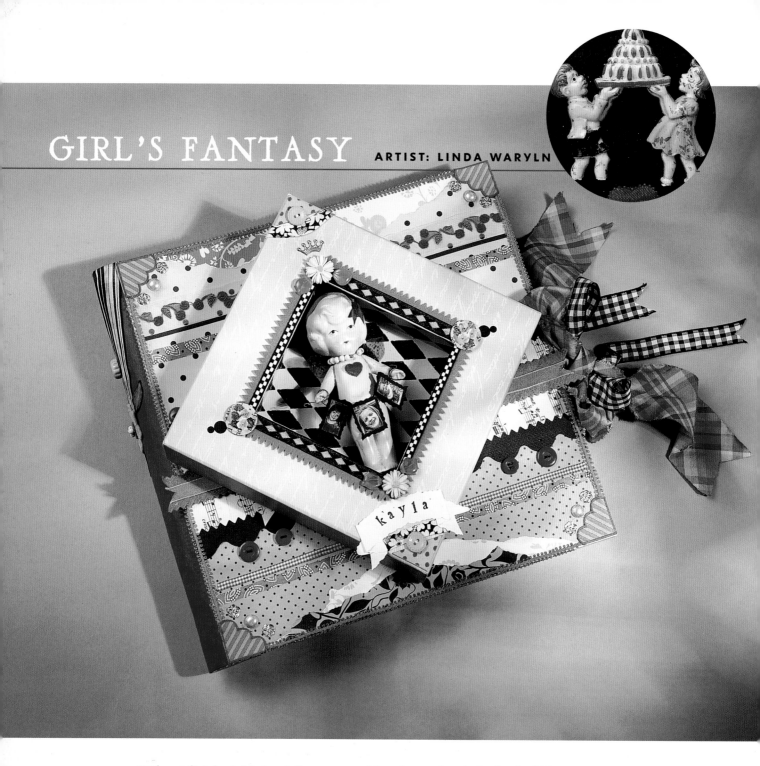

"When I finished this book for my granddaughter, I decided it looked like a big chunk of candy! But that sweetness seems very appropriate. She is almost a teenager now, but this 'little girl's' book is a way of remembering her at various ages. Each page is embellished with a variety of vintage object, mixing the old with the new. And finally, the back cover contains an old-fashioned letter-shaped pouch for hiding private keepsakes." —L.W.

What young girl wouldn't be "wowed" by this handmade book brimming with color and texture! The unique cover features an antique bisque doll in a shadowbox frame. The doll holds small images of the artist's granddaughter, previewing what's to come inside. Vibrant papers, trims, felts, buttons, bows, and embellishments complement photos on the lavishly decorated pages that fold out in an accordion configuration.

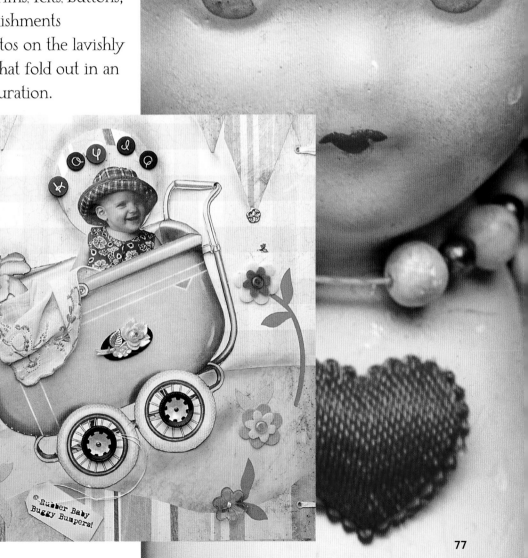

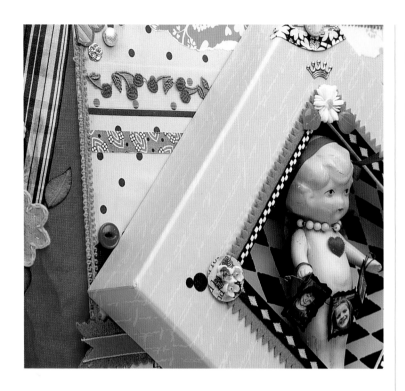

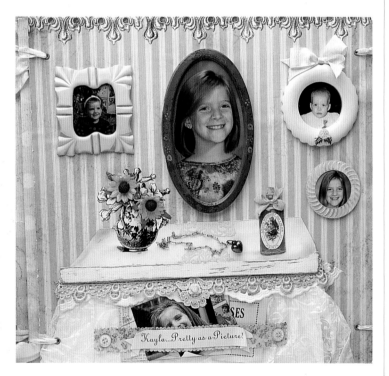

BOOK

- Mat board (cut into two covers and slightly smaller pieces for inside pages)
- Heavy, durable fabric for binding spine
- Eyelets with long shanks
- Medium-width ribbon for tying pages together through eyelets, and wider ribbon for tying together covers

PAGES

- White glue (PVA) and spray adhesive
- Scrapbook papers
- Cardboard shadowbox frame
- Photocopies of favorite photos
- Decorative papers, acetate sheeting, tags, fabric, felts, ribbons, and trims
- Embellishments such as stickers, charms, buttons, plastic or felt flowers, studs, appliqués, tags, scrapbook miniatures, letters, and picture frames

TOOLS

- Hole punch
- Eyelet setter and small hammer
- Scissors

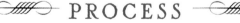 PROCESS

1. Use spray adhesive to cover the front and back of the mat board pages with scrapbook papers to serve as a decorative background. Embellish one side of each page with photos and all the decorative elements you've collected. Punch holes in the pages and insert eyelets.

2. Decorate the front cover with a variety of papers, trims, studs, or appliqués. Linda had an antique doll she liked a lot, and she found that it fit perfectly into a shadowbox frame. She glued reduced pictures

mounted on small pieces of paper to a wire strung between the doll's hands. Adhere scrapbook papers to the back cover.

3. Embellish the pages with photocopies of images and bits and pieces from your arsenal of saved "stuff." In other words—go crazy! Linda's images helped determine her content, and she chose to put them in chronological order on the pages. On the last page, she added an envelope-shaped pouch for holding "secret stuff."

4. After the inside pages are decorated, place them on top of one another to determine the book's thickness. Cut two pieces of binding fabric for the spine, several inches wider than the thickness of your book, so you'll have plenty of room for enclosing your pages and enough width to attach the fabric to the covers. Turn under the narrow ends of each piece of fabric, and place the two strips together facing one another to conceal the turned-under edges. Tack the pieces together with a bit of glue.

5. Lay your covers flat, with space between them that is slightly more than the height of your book, and glue the spine to the inside of your front and back covers.

6. After adhering the spine, glue the ends of two ribbons to the outside edges of the cover for the purpose of tying the book together. After doing this, decorate the inside of the front cover, covering the edges of the ribbons. Adhere some nice paper inside the back cover, because you'll eventually glue down the last page of your book here to hold the connected pages in place.

7. With your pages stacked so each decorated page faces the next and there is one decorated page on top, begin tying them together with ribbons to bundle them in an accordion-like fashion. When you are done, glue the last page faceup, with the eyelets and ribbons on the left side, to the back inside cover.

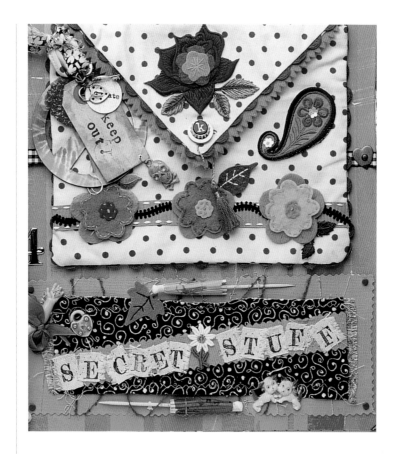

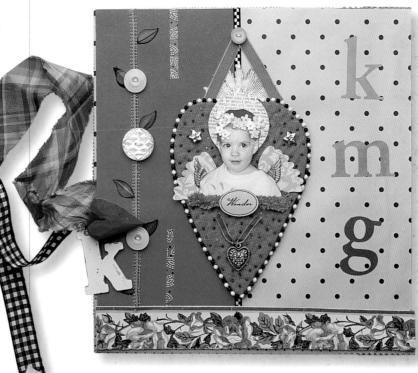

FESTIVE HOLIDAY BOX ALBUM

ARTIST: ERIKIA GHUMM

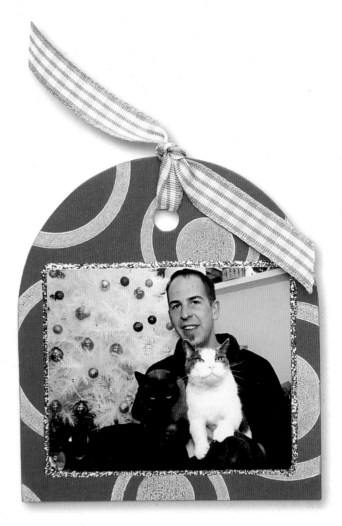

While cruising a thrift store, the artist discovered an irresistible metal recipe box. The purchase sparked her artistic imagination, and this clever idea evolved—a box filled with the eye-opening surprise of bright holiday tags adorned with small photos and memories, each tag as inviting and fun to look at as the next.

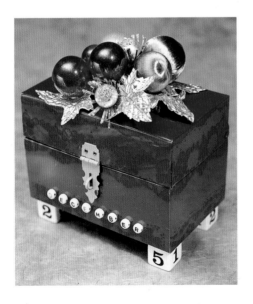

"I had been thinking about creating a scrapbook to fit inside a box, and this box seemed just right to hold pages made from tags. I used lots of digital photos saved from the previous Christmas. I didn't want to decorate the tags with traditional materials, so I worked with others that reinforce the box's uniqueness—such as hand-decorated papers, vintage Christmas decorations, and snippets from Christmas cards." —E.G.

BOX

- Metal box, such as an old recipe box
- Metal clasp and mini eyelets (available at hardware stores)
- Spray paint in red, light green, and dark green
- Doily or other stencil
- Number dice and letter beads
- Strong bonding adhesive
- Calendar page or other memorabilia
- Holiday decorations and cards

PAGES

- Cardstock in various colors and designs
- Acrylic paints, stamping inks, glitter glue, spray inks, and other media of your choice
- Glue stick
- Decorative ribbons (plain, curling, wire), cord, and/or rickrack
- Photo paper

TOOLS

- Computer with photo-editing program and printer
- Sticker machine or spray adhesive
- Scissors or craft knife
  - Rubber stamps
  - Hole punch or die-cut machine

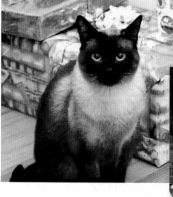

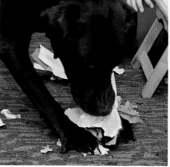

 PROCESS

1. Befitting the holiday theme, Erikia used light green spray paint to color the inside of the box and the metal clasp for the front. To contrast with the lighter color, she used dark green to spray the box's exterior. She used a doily as a stencil and sprayed a red design on top of the green background. Then she affixed the clasp to the front of the box.

2. Number dice seemed a perfect choice to indicate the holiday's date, so she glued them to the bottom of the box, forming little feet. She used letter beads on the box to spell out the month. You can adapt any of this to fit your particular holiday of choice, including gluing a piece of memorabilia (such as a December calendar page) inside the box's lid.

3. Working in a photo-editing program, crop your digital photos to a small size that fits your box, and print them out on photo paper. Decorate the cardstock with hand-painted and stamped designs.

4. Trim the cardstock to a tag size, and apply a backing of sheet adhesive with the sticker machine so you can layer them back-to-back. You can also glue them together with spray adhesive.

5. Use a die-cut machine, scissors, or a craft knife to cut tags from the layered cardstock. If you cut the tags yourself, use the hole punch to make a hole at the top of each tag. Trim the bottoms so they fit into your box. Adhere the photos to the tags with a sticker machine or a glue stick, and frame their edges with glitter glue.

6. On the back of the tags, adhere words clipped from Christmas cards or sentiments printed out on your computer. The words might relate directly to the photo on the front, or simply be a holiday greeting.

7. Loop ribbons, cord, and rickrack through the holes in the tags to add a decorative finish that pops out of the box when you open it. Surprise!

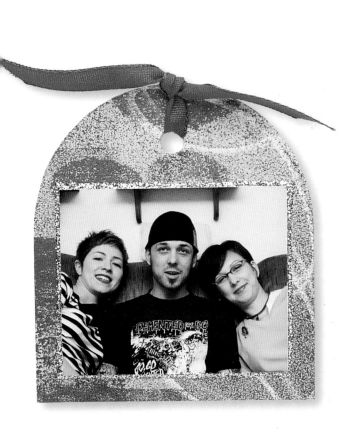

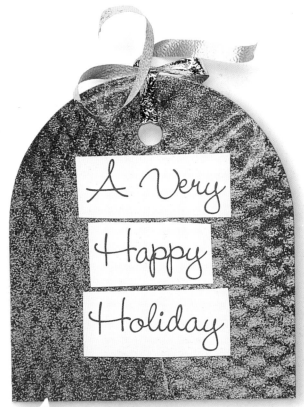

A Very
Happy
Holiday

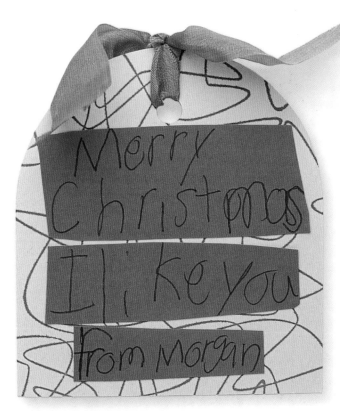

Merry
Christmas
I like you
from Morgan

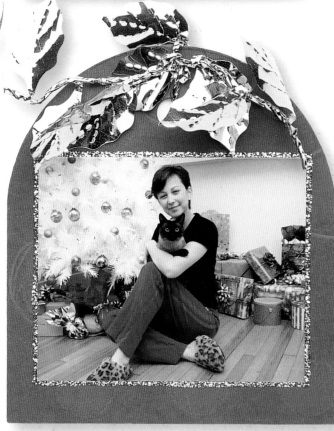

BEWITCHING PAPER DOLL BOOK

ARTIST: LINDA WARLYN

"I love Halloween, and come autumn, my house is festooned with ghosts, goblins, and, especially, witches! This particular witch serves as a decoration while bearing a host of Halloween memories about my granddaughter. Who says a witch can't be chic? A scrap of vintage taffeta worked as a skirt and cuffs. I inverted a pair of paper wings to serve as shoulder pads. A spider's web and charm, paper leaves, trims and ribbons, tulle, and vintage images complete her ensemble." —L.W.

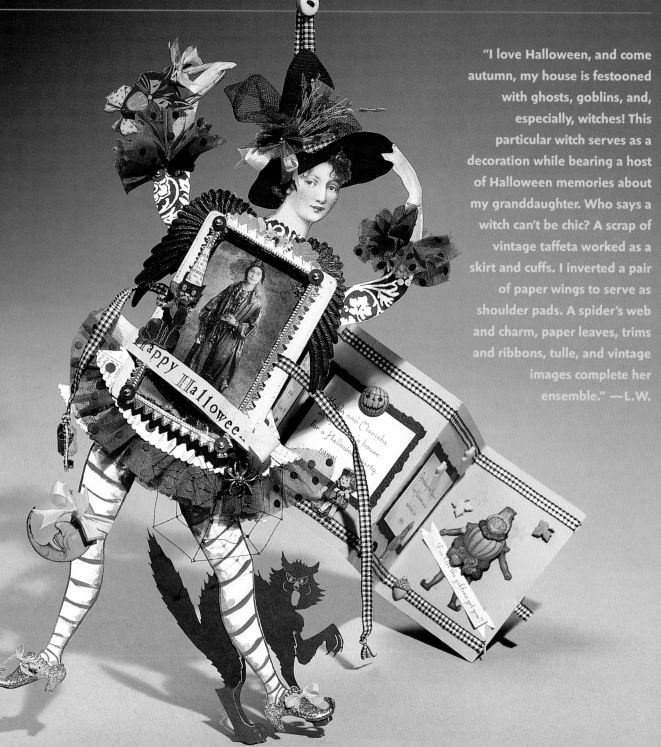

The artist used a vintage image of a dancer and transformed it into a beguiling paper doll witch. Her back supports a small scrapbook that holds tiny images from a memorable Halloween. The torso displays an antique photo mounted on a playing card. Legs are attached to the body with eyelets so they're moveable.

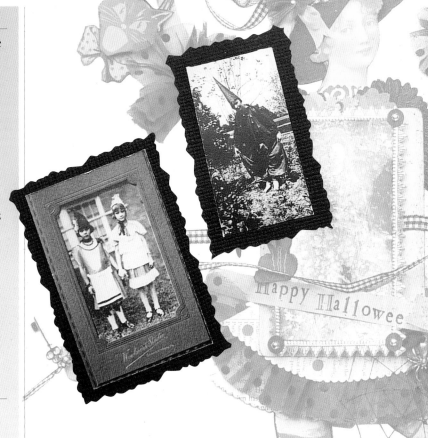

DOLL

- Photocopy of a vintage paper doll (available in paper doll books)
- Cardstock
- White craft glue (PVA)
- Paper black wings
- Playing card, craft foam, piece of mica, Victorian gold scrap trim, tiny stars (for "shaker" box on front)
- Scrap of lightweight fabric for skirt and cuffs (such as taffeta)
- Rubber-stamped images and grommets (for legs)
- Black paper and parchment paper (for hat and banner)
- Narrow silk ribbon (for bows and hanging)
- Small embellishments and trims

BOOK

- Reduced images and photos
- Orange cardstock
- Thin gingham ribbon (for border and tying book)
- Tiny Halloween and autumnal embellishments (available at craft supply stores)

TOOLS

- Hole punch
- Small hammer and grommet-setting tool
- Plain, deckle-edged, and mini-scallop-edged scissors

PROCESS

1. Glue the doll image to cardstock before cutting it out. (Linda only used the head and torso and attached different legs.) She adhered inverted paper wings to adorn the shoulders.

2. Glue the playing card to the front of the body, and add a vintage photo to it. Adhere thin strips of foam around it and drop tiny loose stars or other embellishments inside.

Glue a piece of mica to the foam, enclosing the "shaker" box.

3. Linda framed the photo with Victorian-style scrap, and added tiny circles and stick-on metal dots to the corners for emphasis. She added a small curled paper banner printed with "Happy Halloween" to the bottom of the frame.

4. She used mini-scallop-edged scissors to cut out a paper underskirt for the doll before scalloping the edge of a strip of pleated taffeta and gluing it over this base skirt. She added another paper skirt on top so the fabric pops out between the two layers.

5. You can create the legs and shoes for this doll with rubber-stamped images. Attach the legs to the back of the skirt with grommets so they'll be moveable. Once assembled, glue the entire piece to the back of the card. To complete the front, add Halloween embellishments. Cut a witch's hat out of black paper and decorate it.

6. To make the scrapbook, fold a strip of orange cardstock into an accordion the size of the playing card. Cut out reduced photos and create a running collage with images, a few words, and a border of gingham ribbon on the pages. Linda mounted a few vintage images on black paper and tucked them inside a pocket on the front of the book. On the reverse side of the book, you can label the images with paper placards framed by deckle-edged black paper and add more embellishment to continue the theme. After the book is done and completely dry, glue the back of the final page to the doll's back.

7. Fold the book in place, and glue a strip of gingham ribbon to each side of the front of the playing card. The ribbon should be long enough to tie around the scrapbook after it's folded shut. Glue a loop of ribbon to the back of the witch's hat to use as a hanger, and your witch is ready to fly!

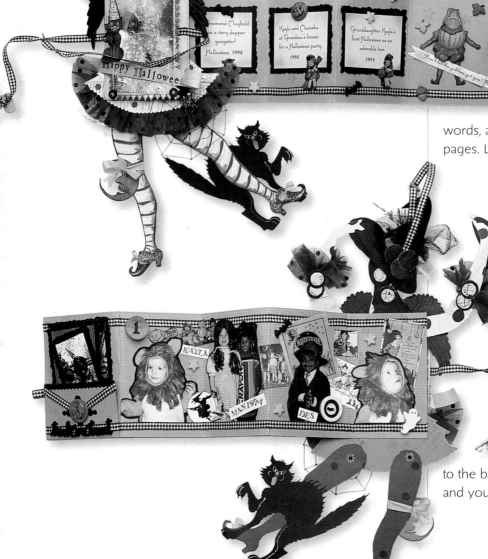

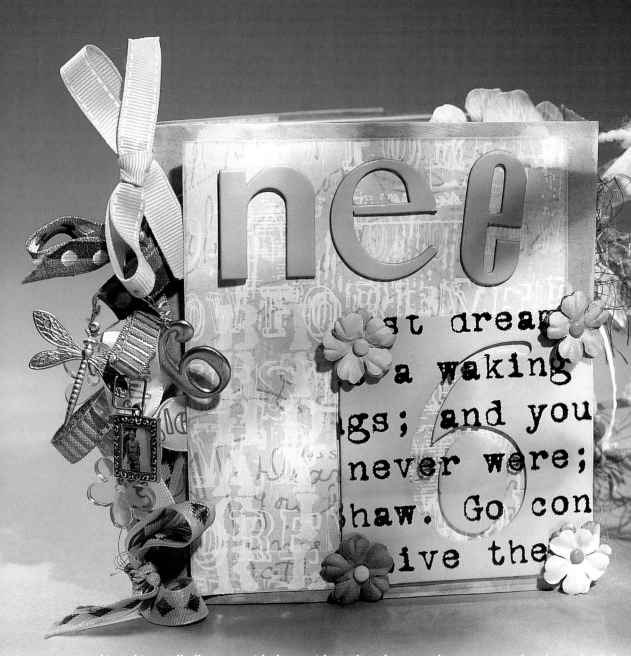

"Making this small album provided me with a relaxed way to document my daughter's birthday. I gathered lots of pictures, and instead of trying to make the layouts perfect, I turned out a more informal and spontaneous book." —G.T.

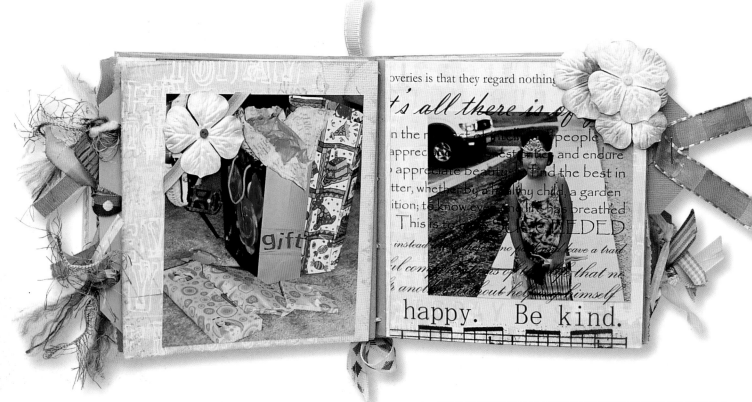

Bows, paper flowers, and pretty papers are used to transform a nifty paper bag book into a celebration of a daughter's sixth birthday. A ribbon binding is tied into place along the spine. Paper tags containing written sentiments are outfitted with fringe and tucked inside the book's pockets, spilling out along the edges.

BOOK AND PAGES

- Several lunch-size paper bags
- Acrylic paints
- Ribbons, paper flowers, stickers, charms and embellishments, brads, and chipboard letters
- Jump rings for charms
- Scrapbook papers
- Photos
- Transparent plastic sheet (top-coated to accept dry toner)
- Rubber-stamp inks

TOOLS

- Awl
- Large-eyed needle for holding ribbon
- Hole punch
- Rubber stamps

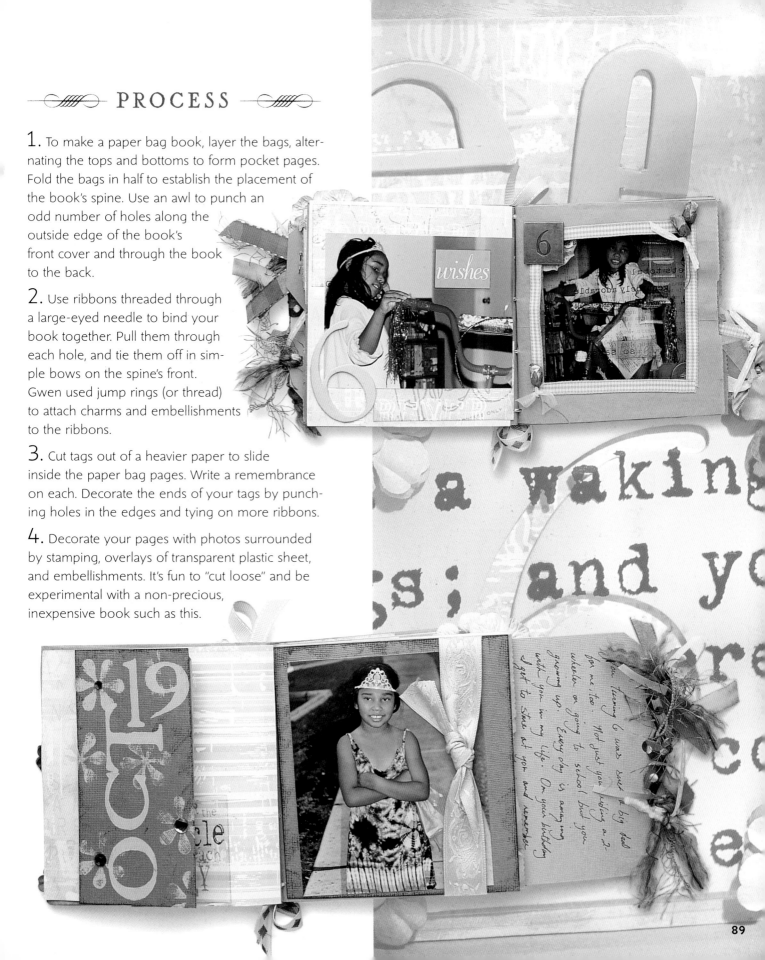

※ PROCESS ※

1. To make a paper bag book, layer the bags, alternating the tops and bottoms to form pocket pages. Fold the bags in half to establish the placement of the book's spine. Use an awl to punch an odd number of holes along the outside edge of the book's front cover and through the book to the back.

2. Use ribbons threaded through a large-eyed needle to bind your book together. Pull them through each hole, and tie them off in simple bows on the spine's front. Gwen used jump rings (or thread) to attach charms and embellishments to the ribbons.

3. Cut tags out of a heavier paper to slide inside the paper bag pages. Write a remembrance on each. Decorate the ends of your tags by punching holes in the edges and tying on more ribbons.

4. Decorate your pages with photos surrounded by stamping, overlays of transparent plastic sheet, and embellishments. It's fun to "cut loose" and be experimental with a non-precious, inexpensive book such as this.

ALTERED HEART CHAPBOOK

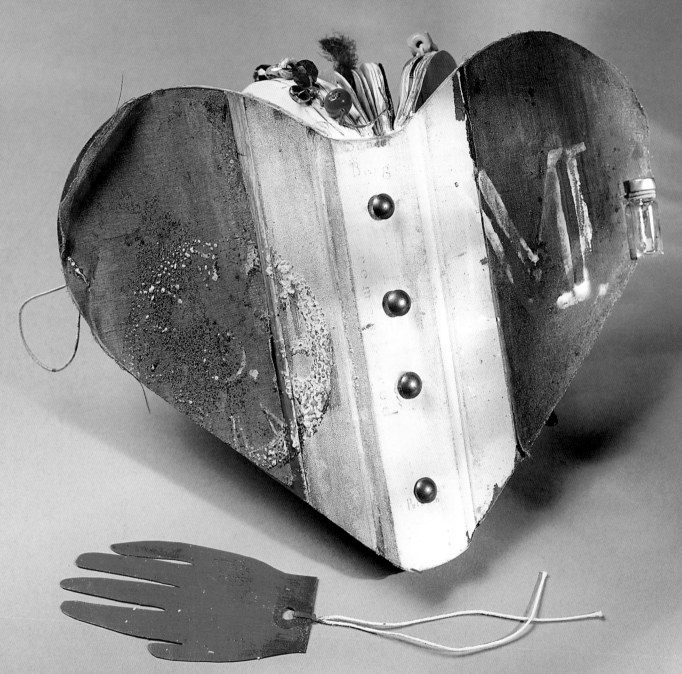

The worn look of this book implies the passage of years, and its shape alludes to its precious and very personal contents. Created with journaling and an altered book structure, the book opens doors to innumerable possibilities outside the boundaries of traditional scrapbooking.

"I am passionate about my family. This journal describes and highlights special moments from past years. When I create books, I want to draw people into each of the pages. The book contains many priceless elements, such as the heart charm given to me by my mother on my wedding day, a coin impressed to commemorate a family vacation, and two dimes held together by a jump ring to symbolize 20 years together. In that sense, this book is very 'real' to me." —S.M.

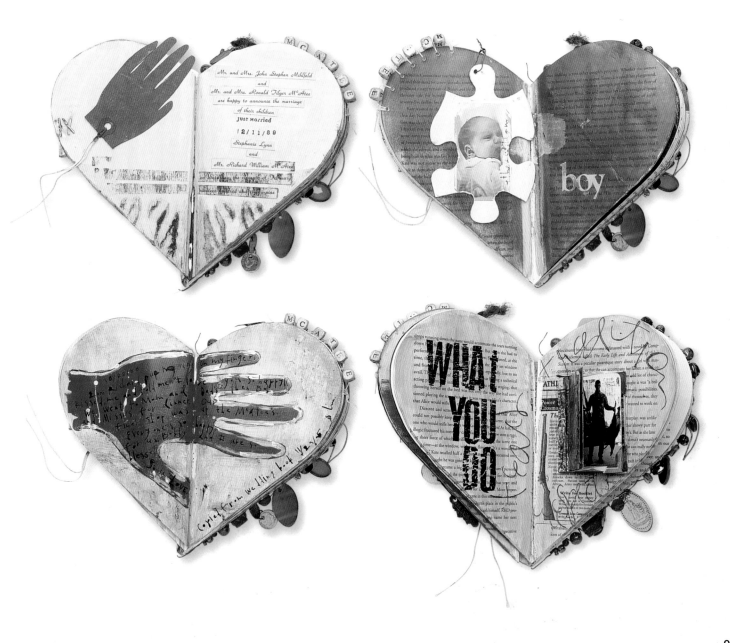

BOOK

- Hardback book cut into half-heart shape
- Wire mesh
- Walnut ink
- Brass upholstery nails
- Acrylic paint and bleach
- Elastic bungee cord
- Small glass vial
- Sandpaper

PAGES

- Acrylic paint
- Glue stick
- Coloring media such as pigmented acrylic ink, acrylic paint, and walnut ink
- Photos and memorabilia
- Playing cards, rub-on letters, wire mesh, and eyelets (for small book inside)
- Waxed linen
- Beeswax and brush
- Wooden alphabet letters, charms, and trinkets

TOOLS

- Electrical saw
- Alphabet foam stamps
- Small alphabet rubber stamps
- Awl
- Large-eyed needle
- Dedicated metal tin, brush, heat gun, and ventilator mask (for beeswax)
- Stapler

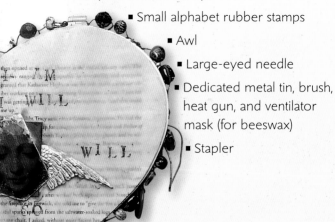

 PROCESS

1. Stephanie cut an old hardback with an electrical saw to create this heart-shaped book. She altered the covers by cutting pieces of mesh to fit on them before painting them with walnut ink.

2. To add decoration to the spine, she pushed brass upholstery nails into the center of it. The letter "M" on the front was made with a foam alphabet stamp and a mixture of white acrylic paint and bleach. She created the book's closure by punching holes in the back cover to hold a piece of elastic bungee cord, and attached a small glass vial to the front.

3. To make your book more stable for holding heavier memorabilia and to take up some of the extra pages, glue some of the inner pages together, as you would an altered book. On a couple of these page groupings, Stephanie added elements to hang outside the book along the curved edge by punching holes along the edge with the awl. Then she attached wooden alphabet letters with a blanket stitch made with waxed linen. On a page toward the back, she used the same punching and stitching technique to attach a host of beads, charms, and trinkets that show on the outside of the book.

4. She used a variety of techniques to decorate the pages, including making pockets by cutting pages with a craft knife and folding the tops down before adhering the pages to form the pocket that holds family memorabilia, photos, and so forth. On another page, she used trimmed-down playing cards to create a small book inset. She distressed the playing cards with sandpaper and painted on a walnut ink finish. She used one of the cards to fold over the entire stack, and stapled the book along the left side. Then she added photos, rub-on letters, wire mesh, and eyelets.

5. Throughout the book, Stephanie added passages written by hand and antiqued many of the pages. For instance, she added the handwritten wedding vows that her grandfather wrote down on a piece of hotel notepaper the night before her wedding. To keep the idea of a personal touch, she traced her hand across two pages and filled the shape with red acrylic paint at the start of the book, beginning the journey through time. She applied hot beeswax to some of the pages.

FELTED WOOL
BABY BOOK

ARTIST: KAREN TIMM

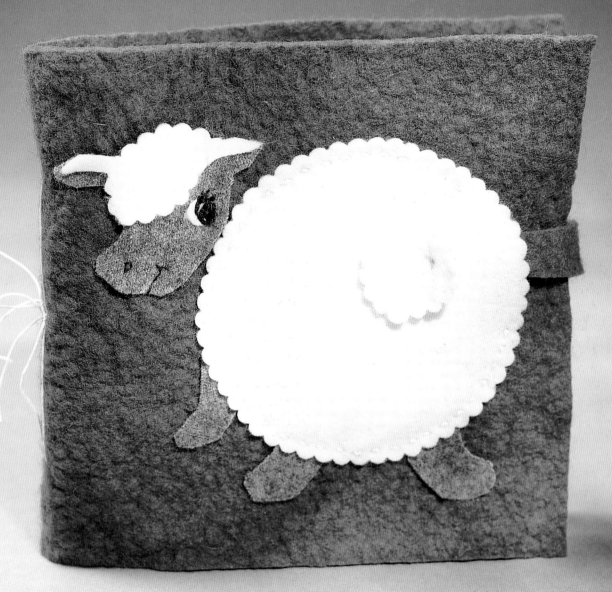

"I like the idea of a thick wool cover for a baby album. It seems a natural choice for the subject, because it is soft, warm, and cuddly. I prefer to keep my pages simple; I believe that journal pages don't have to look busy." —K.T.

The cover for this charming book is made from a piece of wool felted by washing it several times. The cover is decorated with a lamb that invites you to take a peek inside, where minimally stitched pages filled with silhouetted photographs makes a friendly and approachable design. Meandering stitching adds a sense of play.

BOOK

- Old wool sweater or piece of wool from a fabric store
- Pieces of manufactured felt for decorating cover
- Fabric glue
- Perle cotton embroidery thread for decorative stitching
- Irish linen thread for stitching in pages
- Detergent

PAGES

- Medium-weight artist's paper, such as watercolor paper
- Double-sided tape
- Photos printed on heavyweight matte ink-jet paper

TOOLS

- Fabric scissors
- Large-eyed needle
- Black pen
- Computer and printer

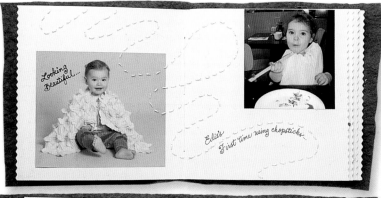

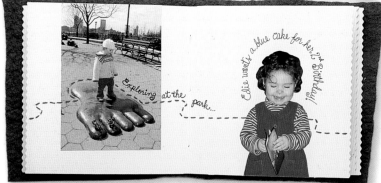

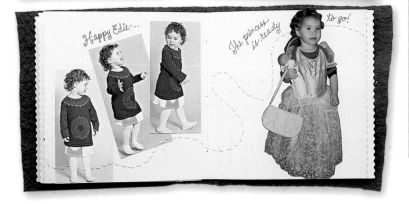

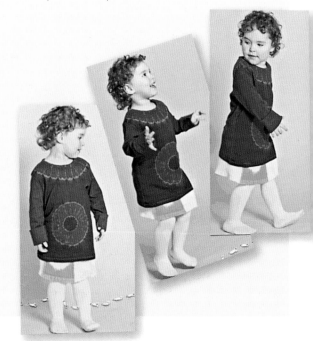

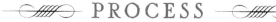

1. You can felt an old wool sweater or other garment, or any piece of wool. If you're using a garment, make certain that it does not say "machine washable" on the tag, because it won't shrink. Wash the piece with other clothes in warm water, using regular detergent. Dry the piece to shrink it, and then clip the wool with scissors to see whether it comes apart. If it comes apart, it's not yet felted enough, so wash it again, this time in hot water. (Note: If it doesn't shrink after three washes, you need to find another piece of wool!)

2. Before working on the cover, cut your pages from medium-weight artist's paper. Karen's book measures 6 x 6 inches, so she cut several 12 x 6-inch pieces from the paper and folded them in half to make two pages each.

3. To make the cover, cut the felted wool, allowing a ½-inch border around the outside edges and a ⅝-inch allowance in the center of the piece for attaching the pages. (In other words, if you are making a book the same size as Karen's, this piece will measure 13⅝ x 7 inches.)

4. Cut out pieces for your cover design from the manufactured felt. It's helpful to sketch something out on paper first, cut out the pieces, see how they work together, and then use them as templates.

5. Use fabric glue to adhere the cover pieces. After the glue dries, use embroidery thread to add decorative stitches to the cover.

6. Before stitching the pages, adhere the photos to them. Cut out/silhouette some of your images. Draw a curved line lightly with a pencil where you'd like to place stitching. Add captions with black ink, following these lines. Punch little holes with the needle along the drawn lines, and then erase them before stitching in and out of the holes with the embroidery thread. You can tie knots or tape the ends in place.

7. To sew your pages to your cover, mark three sewing stations on the inside fold of the pages. Determine their placement by measuring 1 inch from the top and the bottom of the piece, and then halfway between these points in the center. Punch the binding holes with your needle.

8. To sew in a folded signature, use about 13 inches of Irish linen thread. Place the page inside the cover and poke the needle through the inside fold and out through the cover. Push the needle back through the top hole and take the thread through the bottom hole and out. Then sew back through the center hole again. Pull the thread snug, but don't rip the paper when you do. Tie a knot with the ends, keeping the long thread between the knot when you tie it. Trim the thread ends to about ½ inch. Add other signatures, placing them about ³⁄₁₆ inch apart.

9. Karen cut a closure for the book from felt that's shaped like a lamb's tale. She sewed the end of it to the back cover and cut a slit in the lamb's body to slide in the puffy end of the tail. Come up with your own variation of this based on your theme. A button closure works nicely as well.

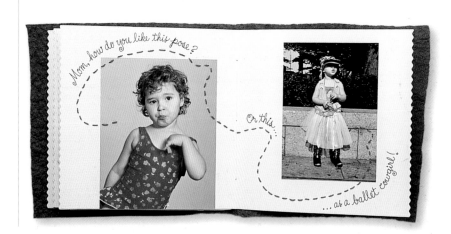

SPORTS CD BOOK

ARTIST: STEPHANIE MCATEE

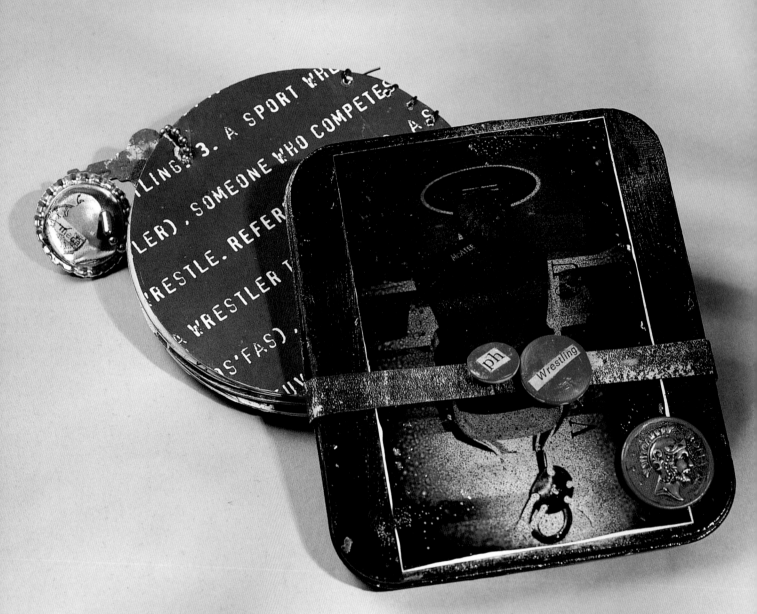

"Wrestling is the one sport for which our boys have a mutual passion. When creating sports journals, you can't really make them 'glamorous' . . . they need to be 'real.' Using rough elements conveys a sense of the moment." —S.M.

A CD book makes a great substrate for a sports theme. The artist cut loose with spray paint, electrical tape, and other everyday materials to make this rough-and-tumble assemblage that thoughtfully captures the triumphs and challenges of competition.

BOOK

- Old CDs
- Metal tin
- Metal bead chain
- Soda pop top
- Large rubber band
- Button pins

PAGES

- Acrylic paints, spray paints, and alcohol inks
- Patterned word paper
- Computer-generated photos
- Glue stick
- Electrical tape and book tape
- Sandpaper
- Slide mounts

TOOLS

- Wire brush
- Glue stick
- Computer and printer
- Rubber stamps
- Needle tool and nail
- Number and letter stencils

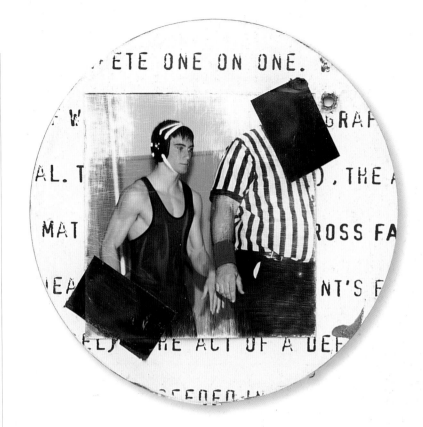

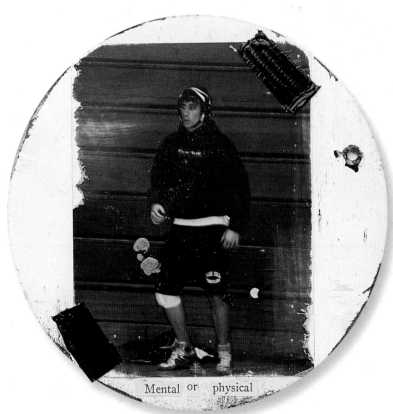

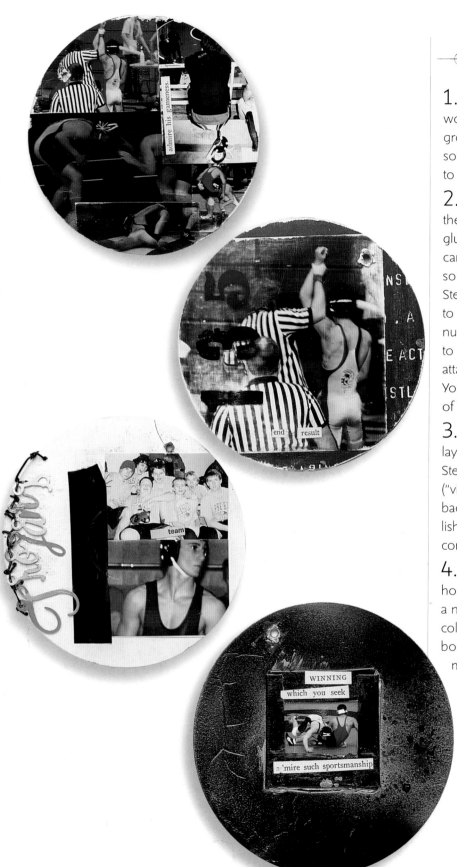

PROCESS

1. Stephanie used acrylic paints, patterned word paper, and alcohol inks to create the backgrounds on the CD surfaces. She distressed some of them with sandpaper and a wire brush to lend them a rough look.

2. When you print out your photos, make sure they are small enough to fit on the surfaces. A glue stick works well for adhering them. You can also use black electrical tape to reinforce some of them and add a masculine look. Stephanie added bits of stamped and book text to some CDs and used spray paint along with number and letter stencils to add a final touch to a couple of them. On the back of one, she attached book tape and stamped on top of it. You can also use slide mounts to frame some of your images, and paint right over the surface.

3. Decorate the front of the tin with photos and layers of spray paint. On top of the tin, Stephanie stamped some appropriate words ("vision" and "quest") that blend subtly into the background. She adhered a "warrior" embellishment painted red around the edges to one corner of the cover.

4. Once the CDs are decorated, carefully "drill" holes in each using first a needle tool, and then a nail. Thread a bead chain through the CD collection to hold them together like a small book. Stephanie added a hammered, painted metal soda pop top to the chain as an embellishment.

5. The tin that holds the CD book is held together with a large rubber band to which she added two old button pins that she painted before gluing words to them.

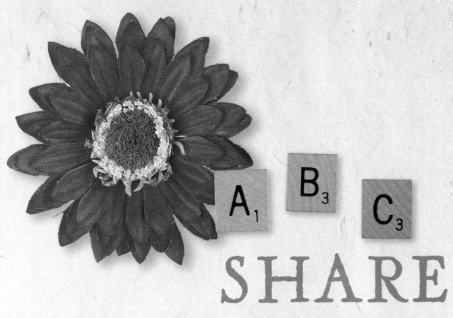

A B C

SHARE

If you focus on what you find beautiful and meaningful, the resulting creation will be a joy to share with others. What is heartfelt is powerful. Share a memory, a hope, a dream, or something that makes you laugh. Sharing part of yourself through a handmade book creates instant connection with people around you.

love

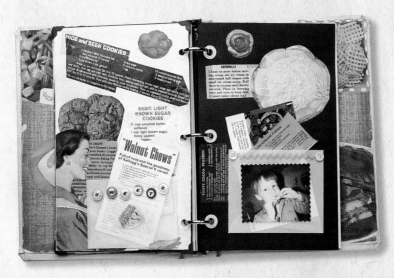

NOSTALGIC FRIENDSHIP BOOK

ARTIST: LISA W. COOK

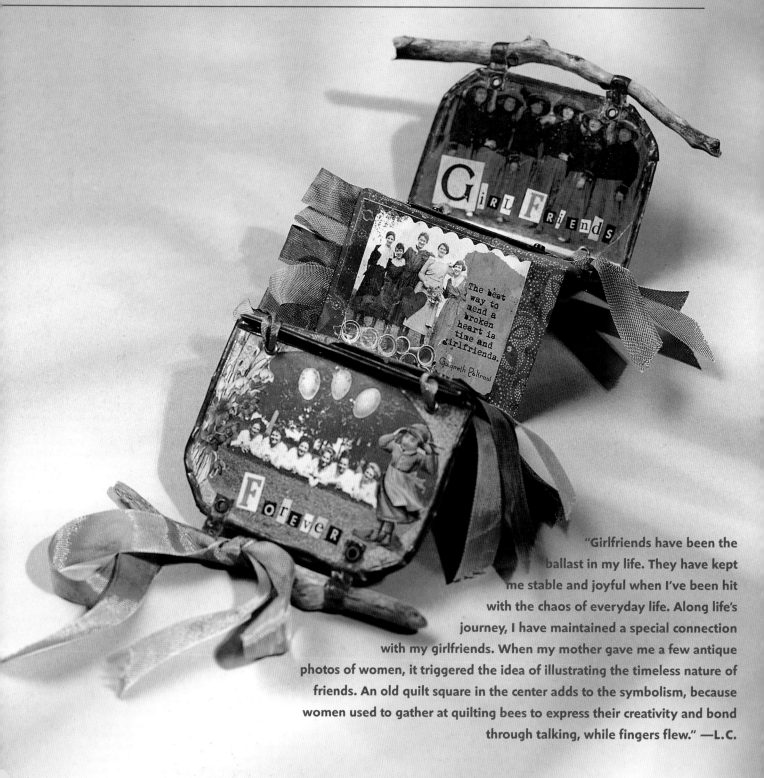

"Girlfriends have been the ballast in my life. They have kept me stable and joyful when I've been hit with the chaos of everyday life. Along life's journey, I have maintained a special connection with my girlfriends. When my mother gave me a few antique photos of women, it triggered the idea of illustrating the timeless nature of friends. An old quilt square in the center adds to the symbolism, because women used to gather at quilting bees to express their creativity and bond through talking, while fingers flew." —L.C.

This folded "book" opens out into an evocative hanging piece that expresses the concept of long-held friendship between women. On the top and bottom pieces, the artist veiled photocopies of old photos with mica sheet to resemble images in old glass frames, and then soldered the edges. In the center, she used a premade quilt square as the background for the central pages. Eyelets and soldered metal connect small worn sticks to the top and bottom.

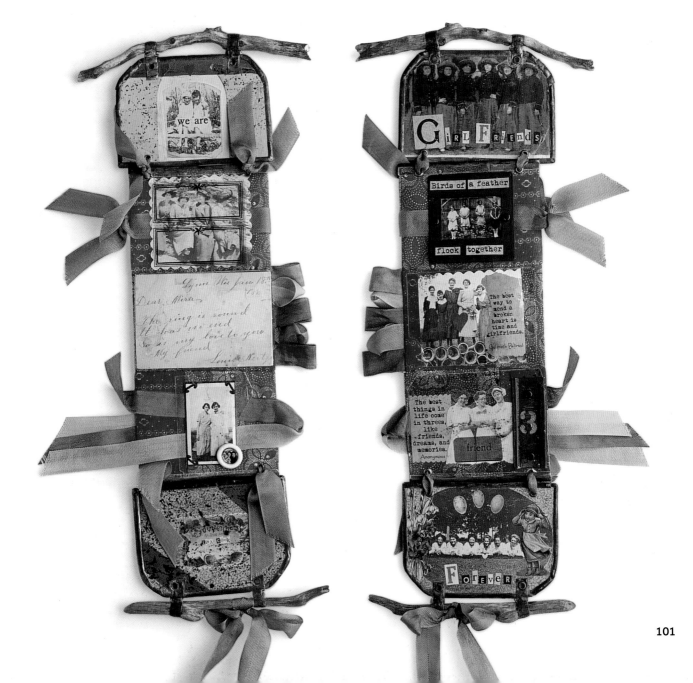

BOOK AND PAGES

- Large sheet of mica
- Black-and-white photocopies, copies of found letters and photos, quotations printed on aged paper, and black-and-white transparencies of old labels
- White craft glue (PVA)
- ½-inch-wide copper tape
- Small worn sticks
- ⅛-inch-diameter eyelets and fasteners
- Stained glass flux
- Lead-free solder
- Liquid flux remover
- Cotton swabs
- Liquid patina finish for solder (optional)
- Quilt square or other piece of fabric
- Rayon ribbon
- Embellishments such as black slide mount and small brass stencil

TOOLS

- Scissors and craft knife
- Blender pen
- Bone folder or burnishing tool
- Flux brush
- 100-watt soldering iron with built-in temperature control
- ⅛- or ¼-inch soldering tip
- Safety glasses
- Hot pad
- Clothing iron
- Small hand drill and ⅛-inch bit
- Japanese screw punch and 2.5mm tip
- Eyelet setting tool and small hammer

PROCESS

1. Mica sheet is easily cut with scissors and can be split open to form identical pieces, so Lisa used this to her advantage to create the top and bottom pieces, or the covers.

2. Begin the top piece by making collages on paper, and then glue them together, back-to-back. Then cut a piece of mica to fit over the cover, and separate it into two layers with a craft knife before sandwiching the collages between them, trimming the edges as needed.

3. To create the back cover, Lisa made photo transfers with a blender pen on another sheet of mica, cut out the image and other pieces, and placed them between a second mica sandwich that echoed the shape of the top piece.

4. To finish the cover edges, you can use lengths of copper tape. Allow the tape to overlap slightly where the ends meet. Miter the corners, clip and overlap the curves as needed, and burnish the tape with a bone folder.

5. Lisa wrapped copper tape around the sticks and secured them to the covers with eyelets. Brush flux on the copper tape, and apply solder with the hot soldering iron to secure the edges. Clean all surfaces thoroughly with flux remover, and use cotton swabs to apply the patina. The addition of solder allows plenty of worry-free handling while contributing to the antique aesthetic.

Safety tip: Always solder in a well-ventilated area. Be aware that any chemicals used in soldering may be harmful to skin and eyes Wear safety glasses because solder and flux can pop and spit. Never leave your iron plugged in and unattended.

6. To create the central accordion pages, Lisa folded a pre-sewn quilt square in half lengthwise, with right sides together. She inserted folded ribbons inside the middle section and sewed the fabric strip together to make a tube with a width that fits nicely between the top and bottom covers. She turned the right sides out to reveal decorative ribbon loops, and pressed the piece gently with an iron.

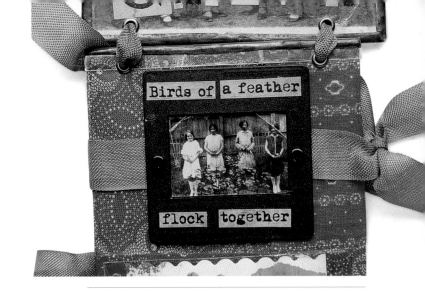

7. You can assemble small collages, quotations, or memorabilia to display on the central piece and adhere them with glue. Lisa found a special handwritten page from a late-nineteenth century friendship book, and adhered a portion of it to the back central piece, adding to the timeless girlfriend theme. Cut protective strips of mica larger than the images so you can glue down the edges to the fabric.

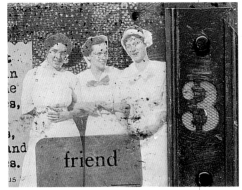

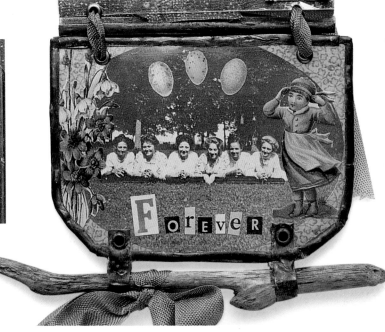

Cover the short edges of the fabric with copper tape and solder, as described above. Attach embellishments to the fabric, such as a slide frame or brass stencil, by drilling tiny holes and sliding fasteners through them to secure them to the fabric.

8. When you finish adding embellishments, lightly glue the inside of the cloth tube together for stability. Use steady and firm pressure on the Japanese screw punch to create holes along the edges of the top and bottom covers and corresponding holes along the edges of the central piece. Set eyelets in the holes, and thread ribbons through them to tie the covers to the central piece.

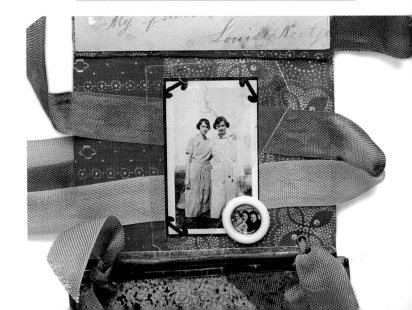

FIONA'S FIRST YEAR

ARTIST: STEPHANIE RUBIANO

"Because my daughter is growing up so quickly, I wanted to document some of my favorite moments from her first year. I admire handmade journals and love perusing them, but I wanted to make a piece that I could look at every day. I created a hinged piece that could stand upright and be viewed as a linear progression. I display this alternative memory book on a table in a variety of formations, and enjoy its story and memories whenever I walk by." —S.R.

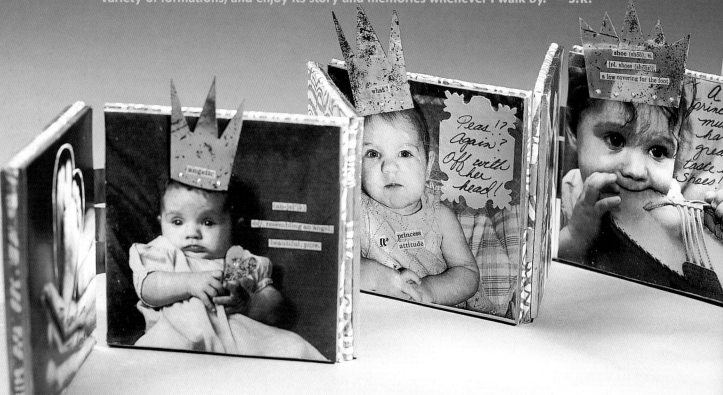

Polymer clay is one of Stephanie's favorite mediums because its versatility allows her to work "outside the box." To create this standing accordion book, she made transfers of images on the clay, which retain the photographic quality of the originals. Some photos are altered with collage or paint. She also carved directly into the baked clay with a pointed tool, outlining certain elements.

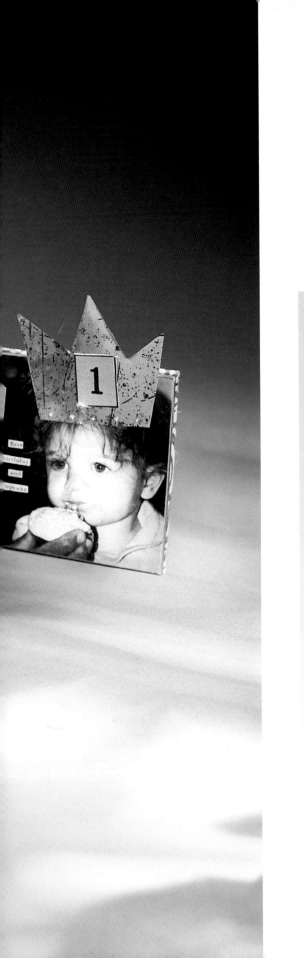

BOOK AND PAGES

- Photocopies
- White polymer clay
- Inexpensive brand of bottled gin (solvent)
- Decorative papers
- White craft glue (PVA)
- Vintage tins or other metal source
- Strong bonding adhesive
- Bookboard
- Linen bookbinding tape or plastic strips from mailer package
- Small screws and nuts
- Permanent pen
- Old book or magazine

TOOLS

- Pasta machine (designated for polymer clay)
- Bone folder
- Oven
- Metal leafing pen
- Utility knife
- Tin snips
- Hand drill or pin vise

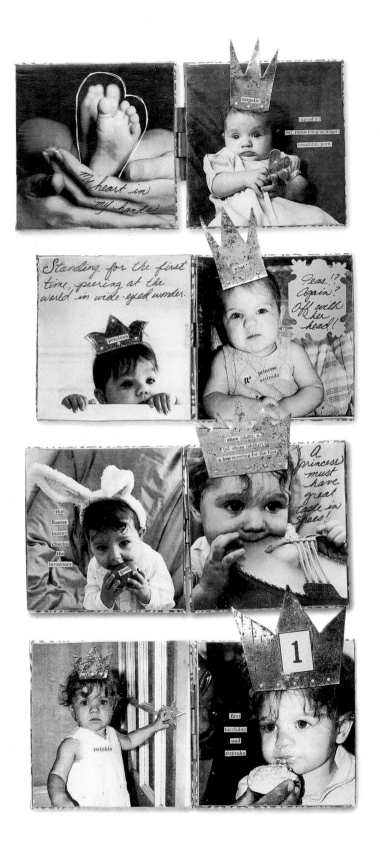

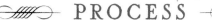

1. Roll the clay through the pasta machine at its widest opening. Place your photocopied images face down on top of the clay, and burnish each with a fingertip followed by the bone folder. Moisten the paper with gin, using it as a transferring agent for the images, and then remove the paper backing from the image.

2. Trim around the edge of each image to create several pieces of the same size, and bake the clay pieces according to the clay manufacturer's specifications.

3. To lend a nice finish to the pieces, Stephanie coated the edges of each polymer square with a metal leafing pen.

4. Use a utility knife to cut the bookboard into squares slightly larger than the polymer ones. Stephanie covered each of these with decorative paper that she adhered with white PVA glue. You can also collage these backing pieces, paint them, or decorate them in any way that you like.

5. If you want to add metal elements to your piece, use tin snips to cut out decorative tin elements to attach to the images. Drill holes in the tin pieces before positioning them on the clay. Mark positioning spots with a pen and drill the holes for the screws before inserting them and attaching a nut to the backside. Clip off the back of the screw and seal it with a drop of strong adhesive.

6. Create a hinging system between each of the bookboards using strips of linen tape or strong plastic from a mailing package. Use strong adhesive to adhere the clay plaques to the bookboard squares and allow the book to dry under weights.

7. Add personal notes and decoration to each page with a permanent pen or collaged words from an old book or magazine.

LOVE LETTER
TO A GARDEN

ARTIST: LINDA WARYLN

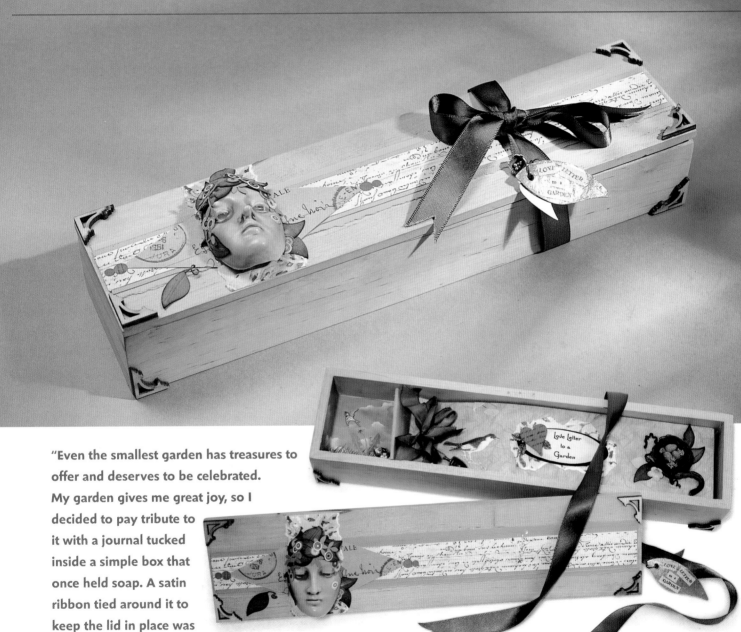

"Even the smallest garden has treasures to offer and deserves to be celebrated. My garden gives me great joy, so I decided to pay tribute to it with a journal tucked inside a simple box that once held soap. A satin ribbon tied around it to keep the lid in place was inspired by the romantic tradition of keeping cherished love letters bundled with ribbon." —L.W.

This unusual piece captures the passing beauty and tenderness of spring. Tucked inside a decorated box, a handmade book holds lovingly tended pages, reflecting the artist's gratitude for her small city garden. Each page provides a different glimpse into a private, ephemeral world.

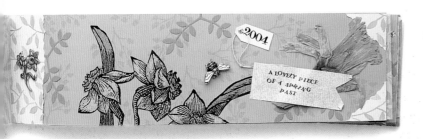

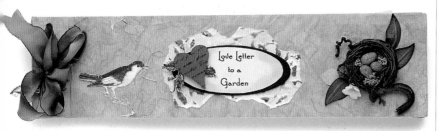

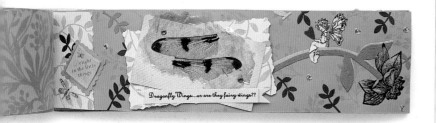

BOX

- Small wooden box
- Dollhouse corner trim (available at craft supply stores)
- Ceramic face (used for art dolls)
- Various decorative papers
- Vintage postcard
- Small piece of basswood
- Small bird and rabbit charms

BOOK

- Heavy paper for book template
- Heavy watercolor paper for covers
- Mulberry paper, decorated vellum, colored papers, and scrapbook papers
- Photocopies of reduced photographs and garden-themed images
- Garden-themed embellishments such as small nest, metal leaf and garden trowel charms, small frames, pressed flowers, feathers, wings, buttons, seeds, and paper leaves
- Watermark ink
- White craft glue (PVA)
- Silk ribbon for looping through holes in book and tying around box
- Glassine envelope
- Eyelets
- Jump rings

TOOLS

- Hole punch
- Rubber stamp
- Deckle-edged and scallop-edged scissors
- Eyelet setter and small hammer
- Computer and printer

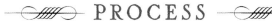
1. After determining what size journal fits comfortably inside your box, make a template from heavy paper for cutting the covers and pages. Punch two holes in the template where you'll tie the ribbon binding. Use this template to cut a front and back cover from heavy watercolor paper.

2. Linda adhered mulberry paper to the front sides of the covers and overlapped the edges to the inside. She adhered scrapbook paper to the insides of the covers before punching the holes. She embellished the front cover with a miniature nest, heart, bird image, title, metal leaves, and other details.

3. Cut the pages of your book using the template. Linda used a light green paper for her pages, and added subtle texture to them with a sprig-shaped rubber stamp and watermark ink. She adhered paper leaves in a random pattern.

4. To reinforce the page edges and provide a pretty touch to each page, use the end of the template as a guide to cut small pieces of decorative paper to adhere to the inside edge of the page. Cut the pieces wide enough for the paper to spill onto the page. Use deckle-edged scissors to trim the edges that show.

5. Glue these reinforcements to the pages, and punch the binding holes in each page. Embellish each page with photos, photocopied images, and computer-generated journaling trimmed with deckle- or scallop-edged scissors. Further embellish and layer each page with charms, buttons, small garden images, various papers, collected garden specimens, and/or tiny picture frames. Cut pieces of imprinted vellum to insert between each page, and punch holes in them to match the pages.

6. For the final page of my book, Linda made a pocket by cutting a regular page in half before adhering it to the page. She decorated the front of it and put photos and a small glassine envelope with seeds inside, and tied it closed with a ribbon threaded through eyelets.

7. Once you've decorated all of your pages, set eyelets in the front and back cover holes. Insert the pages between the covers, and tie the book together with silk ribbon.

8. Linda decorated the outside of the box by gluing dollhouse corner trim pieces to the tops and sides of the box. Then she adhered long strips of torn and cut decorative papers on top of the box. She mounted a ceramic doll's face on top of a piece of a vintage postcard.

9. To complete the box, insert the journal, and glue a piece of ribbon to the bottom of it. Bring it around and tie it in a bow on top to hold the cover in place.

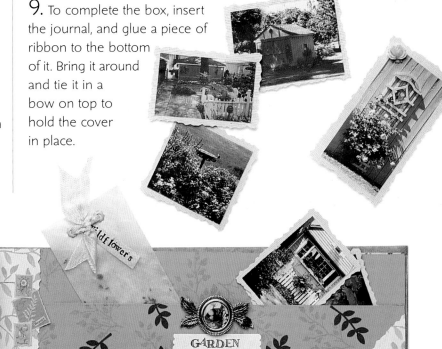

BRIDE'S PORTABLE PLANNING BOOK

ARTIST MARY LAWLER

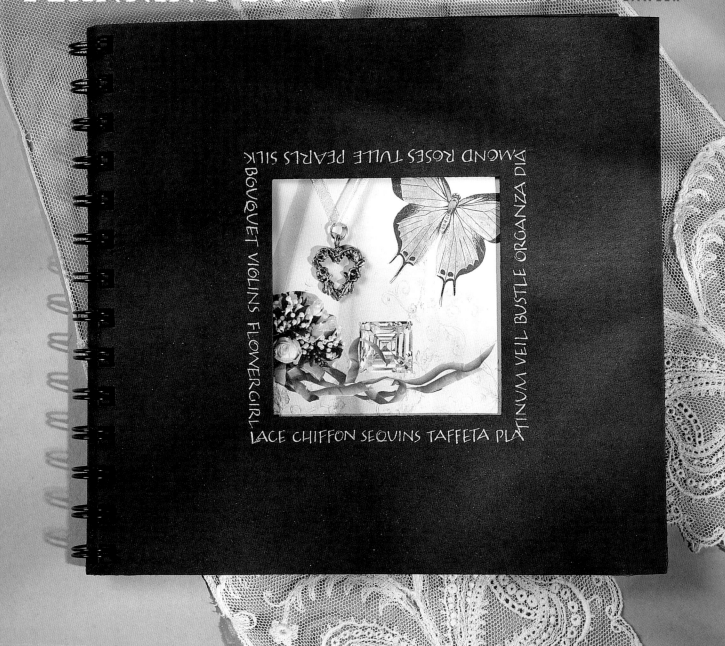

"When I had this idea for a book, I flipped through the first bridal magazine I'd bought in many years and was amazed at how much the tradition of the wedding and its accoutrements still endured: the dress, veil, ring, bridesmaids, cake, music, and invitations. Those traditions are echoed in the word stream of silver lettering on the cover and at the bottom of each page." —M.L.

What bride-to-be doesn't leaf through and tear out pictures from magazines, capturing potential ideas? This portable journal made from a photo album can serve as your visual wish list for exploring color, style, and event ideas, as well as for stashing business cards and swatches.

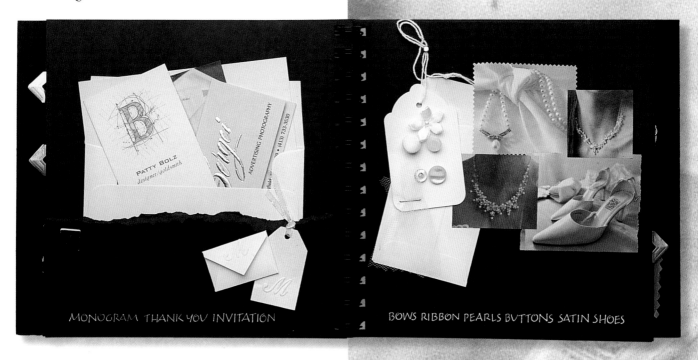

MONOGRAM THANK YOU INVITATION

BOWS RIBBON PEARLS BUTTONS SATIN SHOES

BOOK

- Spiral-bound album or notebook

PAGES

- Photos from magazines or other sources
- Silver page tabs and self-adhesive photo corners
- Adhesive sheet
- Embellishments such as trims, organza ribbons, fabric swatches, buttons, charms, and brads
- Business cards, swatches, and other collected materials
- Tags and small envelopes

TOOLS

- Silver pen
- Stapler
- Decorative-edged scissors

 PROCESS

1. For easy reference, Mary divided her book into sections—such as the dress, cake, and invitations—by attaching the silver tabs to the page edges.

2. As you collect images, stash them in the book, and juxtapose different combinations. Mary began each section with just an image or two that she liked, and attached it with photo corners or pieces of adhesive sheet. Over time she added samples of specific trims, fabrics, or papers that fit the original idea.

3. Use the stapler to attach ribbons or fabric swatches, or stash them in small envelopes. This is your personal workbook.

4. To make a pocket on a page, Mary tore one page in half, discarded the top, and stapled it to another page. She used this pocket to stash things such as business cards or paper samples. She also made notes in the book with a silver pen.

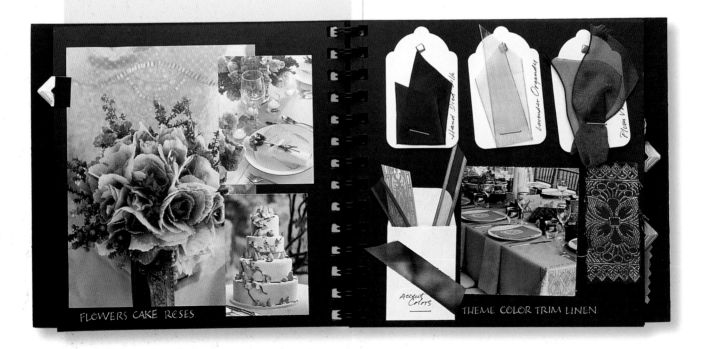

FLOWERS CAKE ROSES

THEME COLOR TRIM LINEN

"UniverSOUL" Circus

ARTIST: GWENDOLYN TAYLOR

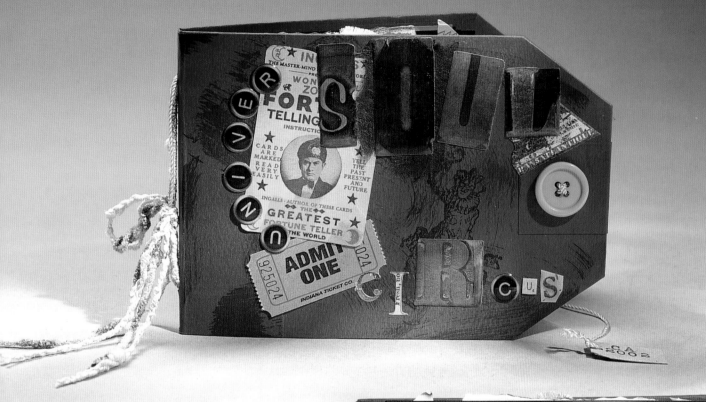

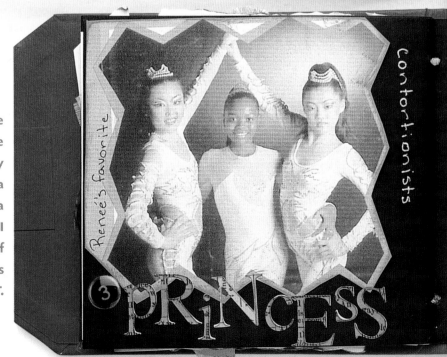

"For the past four years, my daughter Renee and I have flown to Los Angeles to see the circus with my best friend, who is also my daughter's godmother. It's become a tradition, and we look forward to a weekend of relaxation and being together. I created this mini-tag book to remind us of meaningful moments at this always memorable event." —G.T.

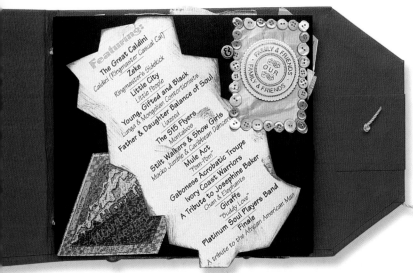

This book documents an annual trip to the circus celebrating a long-held friendship between godmothers and daughters. A fortuneteller on the cover invites you to enter his fascinating and mysterious world. The pages inside open out to reveal the textures and emotions of a fun day of fantasy and entertainment.

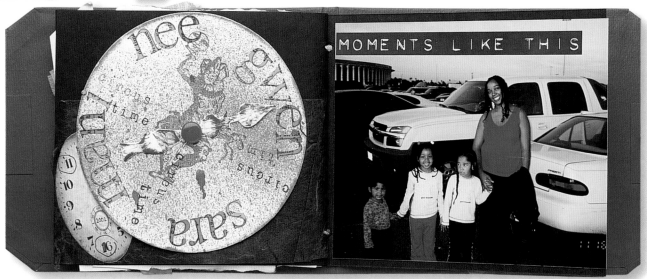

MOMENTS LIKE THIS

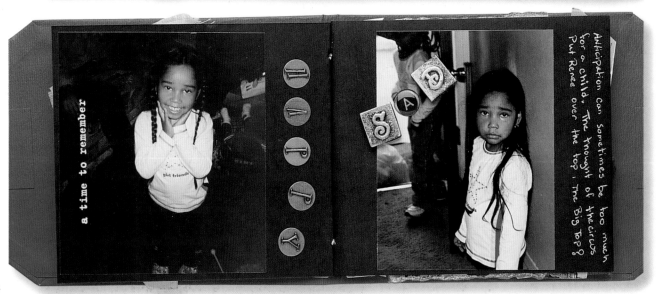

a time to remember

HAPPY

SAD

Anticipation can sometimes be too much for a child. The thought of the circus put Renee over the top. The Big Top?

PROCESS

1. Gwen used a pre-made tag book, because it fit the theme of the traveling circus so well.

2. She decorated the cover with epoxy letters, spelling out her own imaginary name for the group's adventures: "UniverSOUL Circus."

3. Inside she decorated the pages with photos, memorabilia, and some writing. On one page, she rubber-stamped a circular piece of paper with all of the names of everyone and added a moveable hand to make it into a compass.

4. Gwen used mesh, slide mounts, and other common materials to veil and highlight ephemera from her day out.

BOOK AND PAGES

- Small blank book, such as a premade tag book
- Epoxy stick-on letters
- Stickers, die cuts, charms, small tags, and other decorative items
- Event memorabilia
- Photos
- Rubber stamps and inks
- Glue stick

TOOLS

Craft knife or scissors

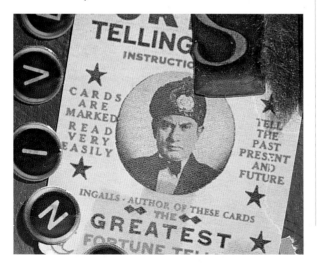

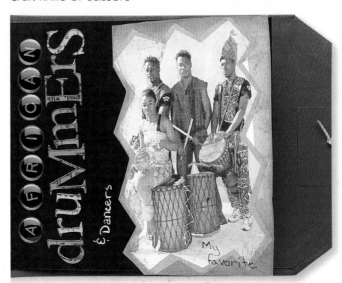

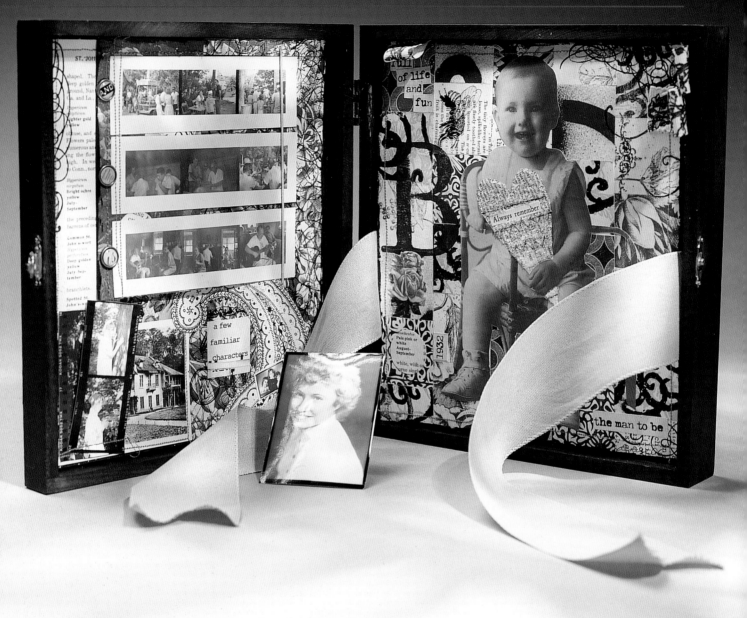

"The collected papers, images, and mementos in this box are gathered from a handful of relatives in my grand family. All of the vintage paper elements in this book were photocopied to preserve the originals, so the pages can be handled over and over. And the box is perfect to hold on one's lap and enjoy looking at again and again." —D.L.

The shape and size of this cigar box is perfect for holding handmade pages. The artist stapled ribbon tabs to the edges of the pages, making them easy to pull out and handle. Although the photos are of particular people, the artist does not spell out a specific story, but invites you to enjoy them as small works of art.

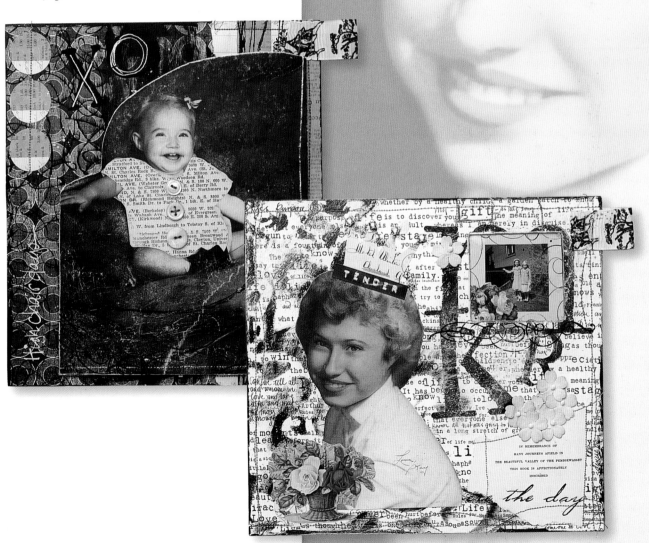

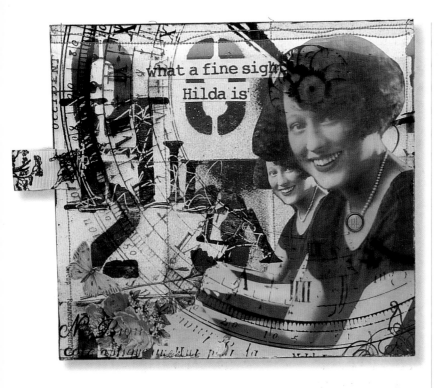

BOX

- Cigar box or other box
- Light molding paste
- Stencil
- Acrylic paint
- Fine-grit sandpaper
- Metal label holder with small photo
- Strong bonding adhesive

PAGES

- Heavy watercolor paper
- Scrapbook, decorative, and vintage papers
- Family photographs
- White glue (PVA) and foam mounting squares
- Acrylic paint, permanent inkpad, black embossing powder, and fine-glass glitter
- Mica tiles and clear acetate sheets
- Stickers and rub-ons
- Buttons, charms, and decorative brads
- Sewing thread
- Ribbon (for tabs and tying the pages)
- Glossy photo paper

TOOLS

- Palette knife
- Paintbrushes
- Brayer
- Lettering stencils, rubberstamps, and paper punches
- Photocopier
- Sewing machine

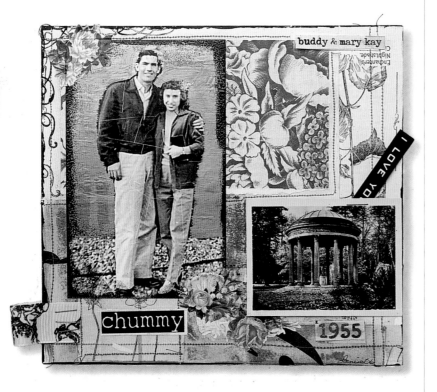

1. Light molding paste is a great way to cover and transform the top of an ordinary box. Use the palette knife to apply it. Texture it by dabbing it with paper towels, and allow it to dry to a stucco-like finish.

2. To create a subtle design on top of this base coat, place a stencil on top and use a brush to add more paste over it. Allow it to dry. Denise dry-brushed the box's top with black acrylic paint and then sanded the surface before applying a buff-colored paint to highlight the texture.

3. Paint the sides and inside of the box, and allow it to dry. To entice the viewer to peek inside, you can place a photo image inside a small label holder and use strong adhesive to affix it to the front of the box.

4. Decorate the inside of the box's lid with memorabilia that relates to the pages inside (see instructions below), creating a visual feast when you open the box.

5. Cut pages from heavy watercolor paper to fit snugly inside the box. This sturdy paper allows you to add many layers of collage to it. Denise used black, white, and cream papers as backgrounds—and to this collection she added family documents and decorative paper scraps.

6. She layered these papers on the pages and dry-brushed them in various places with acrylic paint prior to sanding them. She randomly stamped some of the surfaces, and then spattered gold paint on top.

7. When working your photos, choose a select few, and photocopy them onto glossy photo paper. This paper holds paint and embossing powders well.

8. After creating the base layer, glue on photos, scraps, and embellishments of all sorts, composing as you go along. Use a brayer to smooth out the papers and the adhesive.

9. After everything is collaged and dry, you can add more color and visual interest to the page by machine-stitching around images and along the edges. Embellish the pages with mica, brads, stickers, rub-on letters, glitter, or anything else you wish.

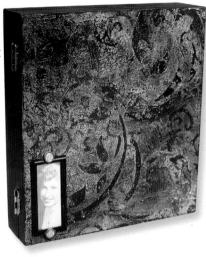

10. Scraps of ribbon stapled to the side of each page add a decorative and practical touch. Wrap a wide ribbon around all of the pages, and tie it to hold them in place inside the box.

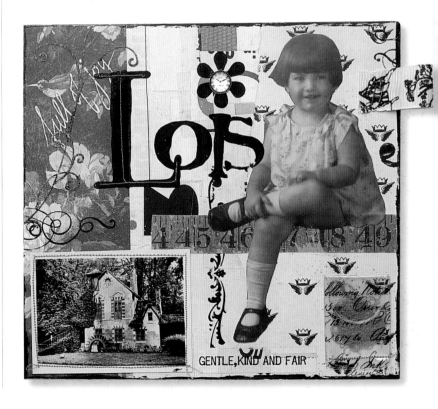

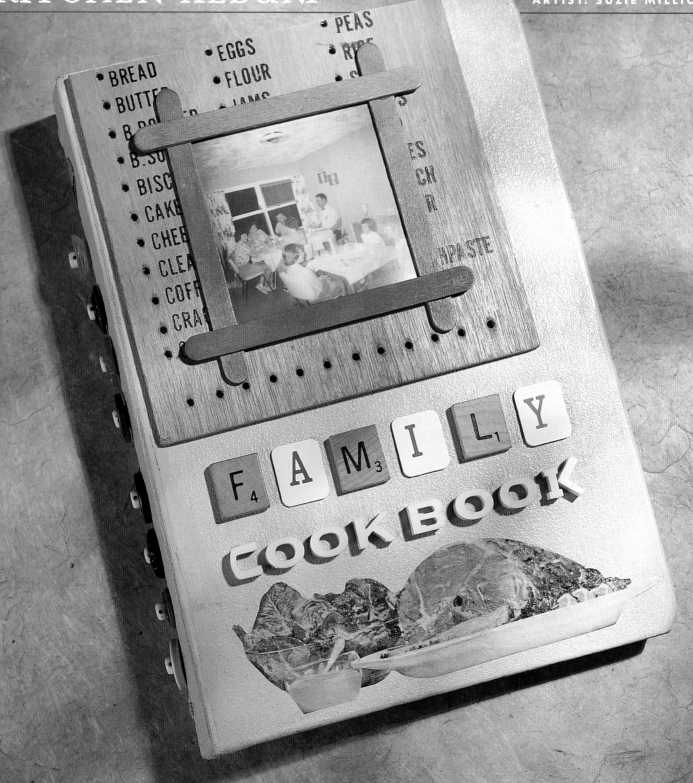

D rawing from her store of vintage photos and materials, the artist pays homage to her family's love of the kitchen, infusing it with a healthy sense of humor! She uses the simplest of materials, such as cardstock and magazine clippings, to create a book that imparts sweet, innocent moments from her childhood.

"This book about my family and our love of cooking contains photos, memorabilia, and some favorite family recipes. I wanted to evoke my small-town Midwestern upbringing, so I used materials that felt authentic, and reminded me of my mother, grandmothers, and aunts. Staying true to this idea, I found memorabilia that might have been scrounged from their drawers, and purchased some others at my hometown stationery store, which sold art supplies, paper, and dreamy office doodads..." —S.M.

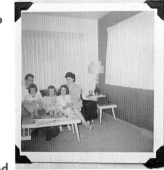

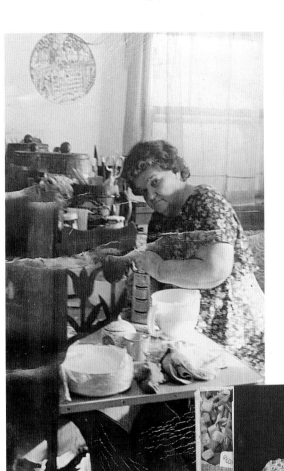

Grandpa Mark's handmade pie counter

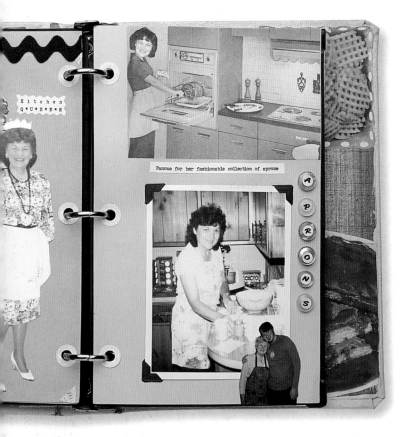

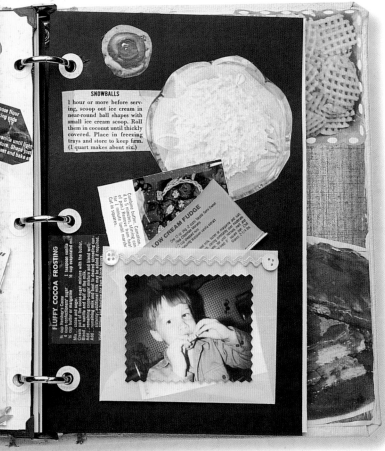

BOOK

- Thrift shop ring-bound cookbook cover
- Cardstock
- Paper hole reinforcements

PAGES

- Images from vintage cookbooks and magazines
- Computer-generated prints from original photos
- Double-sided tape or paper photo mounts
- Embellishments such as buttons, rickrack, old board game pieces, popsicle sticks, paper doilies, pipe cleaners, alphabet beads and buttons, and other era-related memorabilia
- Strong bonding adhesive
- Small vellum envelopes
- Printed recipes

TOOLS

- Computer and scanner
- Pinking shears or scallop-edged craft scissors
- Hole punch

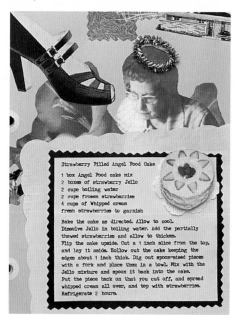

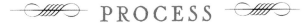

PROCESS

1. The previous owner of this old cookbook had already painted it a pale, chalky shade of pink, and Suzie liked that effect. The retro endpapers were naturally darkened from age and smeared with paint, so she simply added some images of food clipped from vintage magazines to complement them.

2. She recycled some of the magazine clippings from the original recipe pages inside the notebook, and printed out captions in a vintage-style typewriter font on the old yellowed and blank pages of the book. She occasionally shifted the baseline up and down, especially on capital letters and immediately after them, making the text appear as if it were generated on an old typewriter.

3. Print out your own copies of old family photos and images of food clipped from vintage magazines and other cookbooks.

4. To make your pages, cut them from colored cardstock and punch holes in them before strengthening them with hole reinforcements.

5. Mount the photos with double-sided tape or paper photo mounts. To give them a retro look, you can clip the edges of some of the recipes or photos with pinking sheers or scallop-edged scissors. Tuck recipes or memorabilia into small vellum envelopes and adhere them to the pages.

6. Dig into your sewing basket for bits of rickrack to frame images or recipes. Use old buttons topped with computer-generated lettering to create raised lettering and adhere them to the pages with strong adhesive. Sue took this idea a step further and decorated the spine with alphabet beads on top of larger buttons for a really fun and kitschy look.

7. To give the family photo on the cover more prominence, she mounted it on a cut-down portion of an old wooden grocery list and framed it with painted popsicle sticks. To spell out the book's title, she adhered scavenged game board pieces from thrift stores.

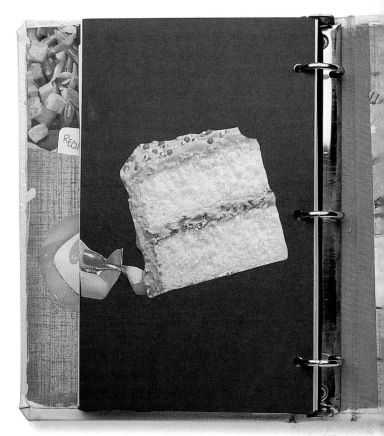

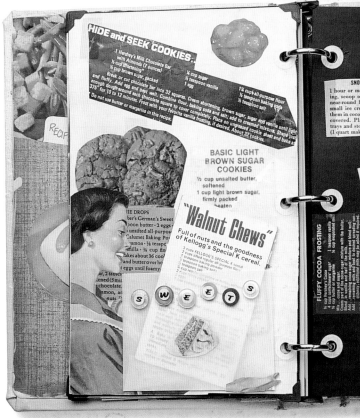

PET SERVICE TAG BOOK

ARTIST: LUANN UDELL

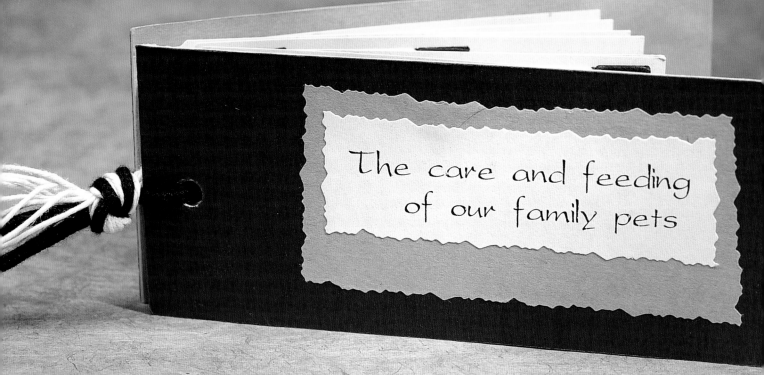

The care and feeding
of our family pets

This clever little book made out of mat board and shipping tags is just the ticket for keeping pet care instructions in one place. It's also a great place to collect impromptu snapshots of your furry (or not so furry) friends—something fun to look back at as the years go by.

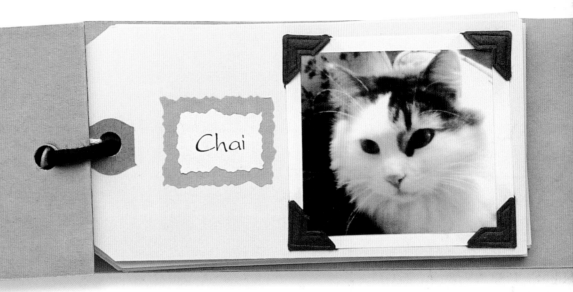

"I designed this little book to hang on our refrigerator for the pet sitter, because we have seven pets in the house! It encapsulates instructions for taking care of each one, along with the pet's name and personality traits. For instance, Bob the guinea pig, loves to have his head scratched, and Greg, the gecko, prefers his cage to be a certain temperature ...they are all so distinct!" —L.U.

BOOK

- Mat board
- Shipping tags
- Cord

PAGES

- Small black-and-white snapshot-style photos
- Computer-generated labels and captions on white paper
- Tan paper for backgrounds
- Photo corners and glue stick

TOOLS

- Mat knife
- Deckle-edged scissors
- Hole punch

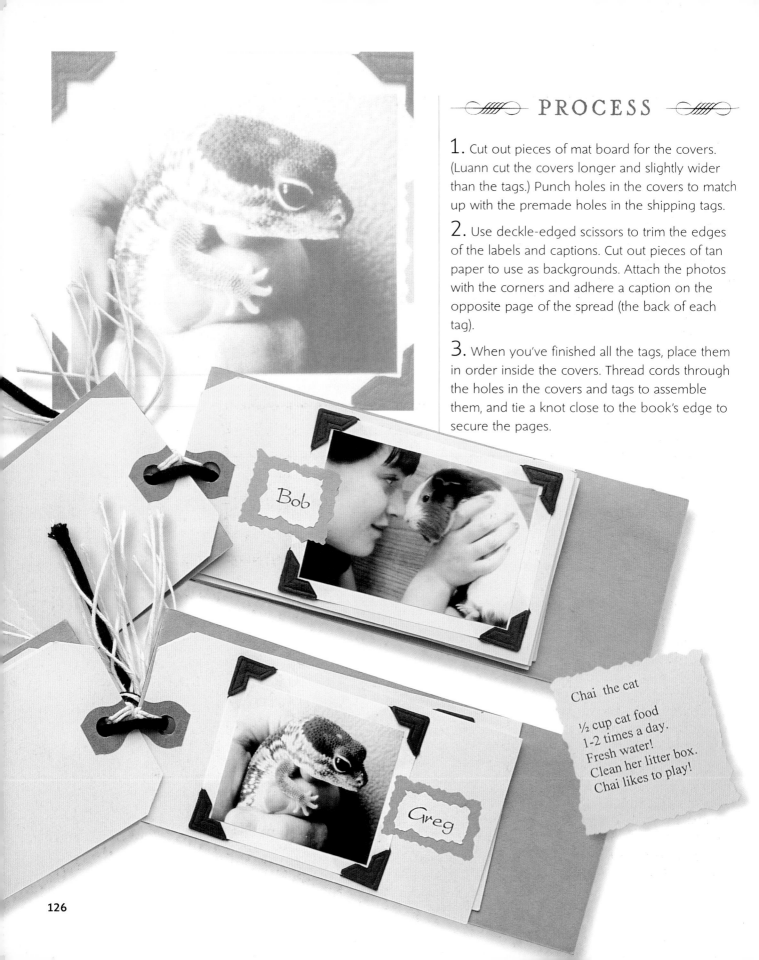

PROCESS

1. Cut out pieces of mat board for the covers. (Luann cut the covers longer and slightly wider than the tags.) Punch holes in the covers to match up with the premade holes in the shipping tags.

2. Use deckle-edged scissors to trim the edges of the labels and captions. Cut out pieces of tan paper to use as backgrounds. Attach the photos with the corners and adhere a caption on the opposite page of the spread (the back of each tag).

3. When you've finished all the tags, place them in order inside the covers. Thread cords through the holes in the covers and tags to assemble them, and tie a knot close to the book's edge to secure the pages.

Bob

Greg

Chai the cat

½ cup cat food
1-2 times a day.
Fresh water!
Clean her litter box.
Chai likes to play!

ABOUT THE ARTISTS

Lisa W. Cook (Amherst, WI) Lisa's love for vintage ephemera is influenced by trips she took to antique stores as a child. Today she combines such elements into highly creative pieces. Her artwork and writing have been published in several books as well as magazines. (www.lisacookstudio.com)

Sarah Fishburn (Fort Collins, CO) Sarah is a widely known collage artist. Her work has been published in numerous art technique books, and she has written for and/or contributed to magazines such as *Mary Engelbreit's Home Companion*, *Memory Makers*, *Somerset Studios*, and *Legacy*. (www.sarahfishburn.com)

Erikia Ghumm (Brighton, CO) Erikia fell in love with scrapbooking because it allowed her to combine her passion for photography and mixed-media art. She is a nationally known artist, author, and instructor. Her work has been published in craft magazines and books, and she has authored/co-authored two books. (www.erikiaghumm.com)

Claudine Hellmuth (Orlando, FL) Claudine holds a BFA from the Corcoran College of Art. She is a nationally known collage artist, author, and workshop instructor. She is the author of *Collage Discovery Workshop* and *Collage Discovery Workshop: Beyond the Unexpected*, published by North Light Books. (www.collageartist.com)

Mary Lawler (South Hadley, MA) For over 25 years, Mary has combined her knowledge of calligraphy with graphic design to create artist's books, mixed-media collage, and decorative arts. She designs projects and teaches workshops for international art supply and paper companies. (www.mindsisland.com/members/marylawler)

Claudia Lee (Liberty, TN) Claudia is a studio artist, educator, workshop leader, and author. Her work in handmade paper is exhibited widely and has been published in books and magazines. She is the owner of Liberty Paper Mill, a working and teaching studio in Liberty, Tennessee. (paperlee@dtccom.net)

Denise Lombardozzi (St. Charles, MO) Denise is a self-taught mixed-media artist who enjoys working in many media. She shares her love for paper arts through teaching. Her work has published in several prominent magazines, including *Somerset Studio*. (www.firstbornstudio.com)

Stephanie McAtee (Kansas City, MO) Stephanie has a passion for collage, photography, and journaling—all of which feed into her bookmaking. She sells her own product lines through her company named Captured Elements. Her personal artwork is driven by her passion—her family. (www.capturedelements.com, www.stephmcatee.typepad.com)

Susan McBride (Asheville, NC) Susan has been drawing and painting for most of her life. She has also written and illustrated three books for children, published by Lark Books: *The Don't-Get-Caught Doodle Notebook*, *I'm-So-Bored Doodle Notebook*, and *Stick It Notes: 100 Doodles to Draw & Leave Behind*. (www.susanmcbridedesign.com)

Nicole McConville (Asheville, NC) Nicole's artwork centers around collage and assemblage, with a particular focus on found objects. When she's not tinkering in her studio or burying her nose in a book, Nicole keeps busy by attempting to play the accordion. Formerly stricken with a phobia for bookmaking, she has learned that even journals can provide a versatile creative canvas! (www.sigilation.com)

Carol McGoogan (Bolingbrook, IL) While pursuing a full-time career in the information technology field, Carol spends her spare time nourishing her creative muse through art. She discovered quilting and fiber arts over 10 years ago, and from there, she has journeyed into other areas including book arts, jewelry making, metalwork, and collage. (cmcgoo54@yahoo.com)

Suzie Million$ (Asheville, NC) Sue and her husband Lance live in a cabin in the woods, complete with a walk-in shrine to Hank Williams! Sue's paintings and shrines have been shown and collected extensively throughout the United States and in Paris. Her work has been featured in numerous publications, and she has just completed her first book, *The Complete Guide to Retro Craft*, published by Lark Books. (www.amerifolk.com)

Opie and Linda O'Brien (N. Perry Village, OH) Opie and Linda are both enjoy pushing the envelope with their unique multi-media pieces. They teach art workshops nationally and internationally. In 2005, North Light published their book titled *Metal Craft Discovery Workshop*. Their work has also been featured in books as well as magazines. (www.burntofferings.com)

Stephanie Jones Rubiano (Austin, TX) Stephanie's polymer clay beads using the mokume gane technique were the subject for an article in *Belle Armoire*, and she has placed twice in *Bead & Button* magazine's national juried bead show. Her work has been published in several other magazines and books, including *400 Polymer Clay Designs* and *The Art of Jewelry: Polymer Clay*, both published by Lark Books.

Gwendolyn Taylor (Mesa, AZ) Gwen was a cost accountant for six years, and a few months of scrapping changed her dreams of formulas and contract negotiations to layout designs and photo ops. She is member of the African American Scrappers. She has contributed to books and magazines, and she also teaches. (www.africanamericanscrappers.com)

Terry Taylor (Asheville, NC) Terry is the author of a number of Lark books including *The Altered Object*, *Artful Paper Dolls*, and *Altered Art*. He is an acquisitions editor for Lark during the day, and a mixed media artist/jeweler by night. His evocative mixed-media work has been exhibited in galleries and museums.

Karen Timm (Middleton, WI) Karen is a nationally known paper, fiber, and book artist. She has sold hundreds of her handmade blank books that have been used to make beautiful scrapbooks and journals. (www.winnebagostudios.com)

Linda Warlyn (St. Charles, WI) Linda is a self-taught artist. Her work has appeared in magazines such as *Somerset Studio* and *Cloth Paper Scissors*. She says that her husband Wally is her biggest supporter in her artistic endeavors. (ldyintmoon@aol.com)

INDEX

Accordion fold, 41

Adhesives, 12

Beeswax, 59

Boxes, 18, 34–37, 81, 107–109

Calligraphy, 29

Concertina fold, 42–44

Creativity, unleashing, 18–19

Embellishments, 10

Ephemera, 10

Fasteners, 12–13

Improvising, 16–17

Memorabilia, 10

Papers, 9–10

Photos, working with, 14–15

Planning, 16–17

Polymer clay, 104–106

Stamping, 11

Stitching, 12, 41, 94–95

Substrates, 7, 20

Supplies, art, 11

Supplies, commonly used, 9–13

Supplies, unusual, 8

Tools, 13

Transfer, image, 104–106

Transfer, on fabric, 32–33